INDEPENDENCE FOR THE THIRD WORLD CHURCH

AN AFRICAN'S PERSPECTIVE ON MISSIONARY WORK

PIUS WAKATAMA

InterVarsity Press
Downers Grove
Illinois 60515

© 1976 by Inter-Varsity Christian
Fellowship of the United States of America

All rights reserved.
No part of this book may be reproduced
in any form without written permission
from InterVarsity Press.

InterVarsity Press is the book
publishing division of Inter-Varsity
Christian Fellowship, a student movement
active on campus at hundreds of
universities, colleges and schools of
nursing. For information about local and
regional activities, write IVCF, 233
Langdon St., Madison, WI 53703.

ISBN 0-87784-719-3
Library of Congress Catalog
Card Number: 76-21462

Printed in the United
States of America

To my wife,
Winnie Muchaneta,
who did all the typing

Table of Contents

The Call for a Moratorium

1

No subject is as controversial and emotion-packed in the modern missionary movement as the suggestion that missionaries stop their activities. This is dividing missionaries as well as Third World Christians both among evangelical conservatives and liberal churchmen.

Because this proposed moratorium on Western missionaries is so controversial, many who react to it do so without a clear understanding of what its advocates mean. This is especially true of those who react against the idea.

Four Main Groups

I see four main groups behind the moratorium. The first is typified by the anthropologists who met on Barbados in 1971 under the sponsorship of the World Council of Churches. They concluded that missionary work was detrimental to the survival of the Indian cultures in Latin America and that it also aided in the economic and human exploitation of the aboriginal population. They therefore recommended that all missionary work being conducted among the West Indians be stopped at once.

The second group is comprised of Christians who rejoice at the success of missions in the Third World. They point to places like Africa where, it is estimated, there are one hundred million professing Christians. They say that since the African churches can in many cases be self-governing, self-supporting and self-propagating, the goal of evangelizing those nations has been met and missionaries should now leave and let the churches grow in their own way.

The third group is typified by the views of John Gatu, the head of the Presbyterian Church in East Africa. Gatu believes that the continued presence of foreign missionaries is now a hindrance to the continued growth of the church in Africa. At the 1973 Conference on "Salvation Today" in Bangkok, sponsored by the Division of World Mission and Evangelism of the World Council of Churches, he suggested that there be a moratorium on foreign missionaries and on funds to Africa for at least five years so that Africans can assume more responsibility in their own church affairs. In 1974 at the meeting of the All Africa Conference of Churches in Lusaka, Zambia, Gatu's proposal was adopted as a reasonable suggestion.

Gatu defended his call for a moratorium that same year at the International Congress on World Evangelization in Lausanne, Switzerland. "There will never be a real relationship between the African churches and Western missionaries," he said, "because the missionaries regard Africans as ecclesiastical children." His call was echoed by a number of other evangelical leaders. However, the majority of the participants, including Billy Graham, rejected the idea of a moratorium. But Graham did admit that there may be some places in the world where the church would actually be stronger if missionaries were withdrawn and sent to areas of greater need.

Others rejecting a moratorium were African leaders Samuel Odunaike of Nigeria, who is the president of the Association of Evangelicals of Africa and Madagascar, retired Archbishop

Erica Sabiti of Uganda and Dr. Byang Kato, who was, until his recent death, General Secretary of the Association of Evangelicals of Africa and Madagascar.

What is rather significant is that even though these gentlemen rejected a moratorium on spiritual, scriptural and practical grounds, they did not feel free to speak to the issues which led Gatu to conclude that a moratorium is needed. They were rightly concerned about scriptural, political and economic ramifications of such a moratorium, but this does not exempt them from dealing frankly with deteriorating relationships between Western missions and national churches.

The fourth group, with whom I identify, advocate a selective moratorium. This large segment holds that only those with particular social and cultural and spiritual qualifications should go overseas as missionaries to meet specific needs, especially in the area of training nationals at a higher level.

Missions from Both Sides

It is my intention in this book to discuss from a personal perspective, the historical milieu out of which the call for moratorium comes, the mood of its proponents as well as its possible effects on the Third World. My first three chapters take up in turn the first three groups advocating a moratorium. The remainder of the book outlines the directions I feel missionary work should take in pursuing a selective moratorium.

I feel my background qualifies me to write about Third World missions from a personal and an African perspective. I am a product of missions, having accepted Christ as a teenager while training to be a teacher at an evangelical mission station. After graduating from that teacher training school I have worked very closely with missionaries in various capacities.

I have seen missions from the other side as well. I spent four years of study in the United States at an evangelical institution with a strong missionary emphasis. I also visited many mission-supporting evangelical churches, especially in the

American Midwest. I discussed missions both with mission-
aries from other parts of the world on furlough in the United
States and with international students from all parts of the
Third World.

It was the issue of moratorium which prompted me to write
this book. But I have not confined myself to that issue alone.
Instead, it is the central theme around which I discuss other
issues confronting missionary work today.

Moratorium to Preserve Cultures

2

It was at the Barbados meeting of anthropologists in 1971 that the suggestion first gained prominence that missions should stop their work among the Indians of Latin America. This group charged missionaries with destroying indigenous cultures and helping to exploit native populations for the benefit of the West. Although I believe these men are ultimately wrong for scriptural and other reasons, it is worthwhile asking if there is any substance to the charge.

A Dressed Up Gospel

It must be admitted that in preaching the gospel message, missionaries have not been entirely without fault. However, the charge of the Barbados Declaration is misdirected. The problem is not that missionaries are changing cultures but that they are failing to adapt the naked gospel to different cultures. Often the gospel has been transported to other countries wrapped with the cumbersome paraphernalia of Western culture. This has not only retarded indigenous expressions of the

Christian faith, but at times it has unnecessarily caused confusion in and harm to existing social structures.

Because of ignorance as well as ethnic pride, missionaries have often exhibited a negative attitude toward other cultures. They have looked on them as aberrations, their own being the norm. In some cases, they have followed the example of the Judaizers in the early church, insisting that other people take on their cultural ways upon becoming Christians.

In many parts of Africa today, African names are called "heathen" and English names are referred to as "Christian." In the January 1974 issue of *International Review of Mission,* Ezekiel Makunike writes,

> Since it was believed that Christianity could not find a home within the existing African cultural values, the church had tended to take the stronger affecting role. Take for example, the question of names. My own father's African name was Mangombe, meaning "one who owns a large head of cattle." When he became a Christian, he was baptised Charles. My mother's name was Pfumai, meaning "may thou be wealthy." When she became a Christian she was given the name of Helen.

Traditional African dress is also "heathen" and Western dress "Christian." Many missionary presentations shown to church audiences in America picture the "heathen" wearing traditional native dress. The same person is then shown after he becomes a Christian and guess what! He is now wearing a shirt, tie and pants. His spiritual conversion is thus depicted by a change from native dress to Western dress.

The missionaries condemned most traditional rites of passage and social ceremonies as pagan without any prior study to discover whether the meaning behind those ritual forms was, in fact, contrary to the teachings of Scripture. They exhorted Africans to keep away from these rites and ceremonies which the missionaries considered defiling. Christians who participated were fired if they were in mission employ or disciplined if they were only church members. In many cases these condemned "heathen practices" are no different from the laying of wreaths, the saluting of the flag, the firing of a volley at a soldier's funeral, sitting on Santa's lap, or the tricking and treating at Halloween that most Christians innocently participate in, in the Western world.

For example, traditional music and the dancing that accompanies it in Africa was rejected as "heathen." African Christians were required to sing hymns imported from Europe and America which were set to unfamiliar and, therefore, hardly singable music. The basic African musical instruments, the drum, xylophone and rattle, were not allowed into churches or Christian schools. Many African teachers lost their jobs or were censored for permitting their pupils to dance to innocent folk music.

Because of all these errors, should we then call on missionaries to go home and on those considering missionary work overseas to stay at home? There is another solution. Christian colleges and missionary training schools are well aware of the problem. They are offering courses in biculturalism and cross-cultural communications to help missionaries take only the gospel of salvation to other parts of the world without insisting that new believers also assimilate Western culture. Hopefully, they will also encourage nationals to cultivate those things which are wholesome in their own cultural patterns.

Exploitation, Colonization and Education

What of the accusation from Barbados that missions help to exploit native populations? It is true that historically missions were part and parcel of the colonizing process of African and other Third World countries. In some cases missionaries shared the same imperialistic ambitions that the rest of their countrymen had. Many, therefore, actively participated in the colonization of Africa and Asia. Still, the accusation is too broad a generalization.

Despite the negative side of missionary involvement in colonization, we should thank God that missionaries were involved. They helped in tempering the cruel excesses of their
countrymen and in many cases pleaded successfully for the
rights of indigenous populations. Some of them stood up for
nationals at great cost.

In order to teach Christianity and to bring the benefits of
Western civilization to people they considered uncivilized,
missionaries introduced schools. Sometimes they did this
despite much opposition from the colonial governments which
regarded and treated nationals as worthless and inferior
beings to be exploited as cheap labor.

Because many Africans accepted the Christianity they read
about in the Bible, they gained a sense of worth and dignity in
the face of degradation by their colonial masters when otherwise they would have been crushed with feelings of inferiority.
The Bible freed them spiritually and also socially by giving
them a sense of equality with other races. The Bible assured
them that they were created in God's image and were important enough in God's sight for Christ to die for them. As the
deeper implications of these truths were understood, the struggle for political, social and economic freedom was on. It is therefore an indisputable fact that in Africa, at least, the struggle
for self-determination was a direct result of missionary work.
Most of the leadership of today's independent Africa was
educated in mission schools.

Christ in Cultures
Before leaving this topic, I would like to look at the sociological
and the biblical evidence on the issue. The thesis that cultures
must be left intact in order to be indigenous rejects the basic
anthropological and sociological principle of the essential
plasticity of culture. Cultures everywhere, by their very
nature, are undergoing change in adapting to new environments and by coming into contact with other cultures.

Even without external stimuli cultures change because the human being is by nature innovative. He is constantly inventing better methods and tools to enhance the quality of his existence. There is no such thing as a culture which is intact except for those of past civilizations studied by historians and archaeologists. Since their architects are dead, they can no longer change. Living cultures, however, are not static. They will continue to change for better or worse with or without the presence of missionaries.

Unfortunately some churches lost their missionary vision because of this wrong thinking. The reason is not far to find. To say that evangelism must be stopped because it is changing people's cultures is dangerous since it is in direct disobedience to the Lord's command to "go into all the world." The idea of preserving cultures is good, but we must be careful that we do not regard cultures as sacred. Men's souls are more important than their cultures.

Thus many no longer believe that man is lost and in need of salvation. This has its roots in a liberal theology which rejects the authority of the Bible as the inspired and inerrant Word of God. Being puffed up in their own knowledge, they deny the deity of Christ and the lostness of man as taught in the Scriptures. Indeed they question anything which does not agree with their own finite reasoning.

The Bible says "all have sinned and fall short of the glory of God" (Rom. 3:23). Salvation comes to man only through the gospel of Jesus Christ. People can accept this gospel only if they hear it. The only way they can hear is for missionaries to be sent wherever sinful man may be found. The Bible honors missionaries and even calls their feet beautiful (Rom. 10:13-15).

In the light of these facts it is foolish for anybody to say missionary work should come to a halt. Rather, the emphasis should be laid on the necessity of missionaries to learn from their past mistakes and to listen to national voices. Above all they must have the proper cultural and social qualifications as well as spiritual qualifications to enable them to work in other cultures effectively. The training of cross-cultural missionaries is discussed in a later chapter.

Moratorium Because of Success

3

The success of missions overseas is a fact. It is estimated that in the once dark continent of Africa there are now over one hundred million professing Christians. In Asia and other areas of the Third World literally thousands are being added to the family of God every day. In Latin America the church is growing even faster than the birth rate.

Churches planted by Western missionaries have taken root in the indigenous soils and are in turn bearing much fruit. They have dedicated pastors, evangelists and lay leaders who are filled with the Holy Spirit and who are proclaiming the good news of salvation through Christ without fear or shame. Some have vigorous programs of their own and are sending and supporting their own missionaries who are going to unreached areas around them.

Because of the apparent growth of the church overseas, some are saying missionaries should now stop going to these countries and let nationals do the remainder of the evangelism. They feel that the Third World churches should be self-governing, self-supporting, self-propagating and self-instructing without outside interference from foreign missionaries. Others feel that the sending countries should now stop providing missionaries but continue to send money to indigenous churches and mission groups which can do the job far better than foreigners.

Only One Limitation

It is true that many mission-founded churches in Africa and other parts of the world can continue to grow without the presence of foreign missions. God's work does not depend on man's wisdom or organization but on God's Spirit. When the Italians invaded Ethiopia in 1935, all missionaries left the country leaving a handful of believers behind. When the Italians were driven out by the British and Ethiopians in 1941, the missionaries returned. They were amazed at what had happened in their absence. The handful of believers had multiplied to a multitude of several thousands!

However, the fact that churches can exist and grow without the presence of foreign missionaries is not a compelling reason why missionaries should stop going overseas. Matthew 28: 19-20 gives only one limitation to the Great Commission. We should go until the end of the age. This clearly means that Christ expects missionary work across cultures to continue until his return. He did not command his followers to go until churches became self-governing, self-supporting and self-propagating. Until he returns, therefore, missionaries will be needed in all parts of the world including the United States.

During my stay in America I noticed that most of the large mission boards sending missionaries overseas have no outreach at home. In Luke 24:47, the Lord commanded the disciples to go into all the world but to start at Jerusalem, their own home.

The assumption that the missionary is one who goes overseas is erroneous. The Lord calls some to labor at home where the fields are equally "ripe unto harvest." In fact, I question the sincerity of those who have no concern at all for the salvation of pagan American blacks, Chicanos, whites, Indians and others, but will cross oceans to reach and love these same people in other parts of the world.

The idea of stopping men and women from working in areas to which they feel called by God is not biblical. It negates the whole concept of the church being the body of Christ we read about in 1 Corinthians 12. As members of one body we should be free to minister to the world and to one another across geographic, racial, ethnic, cultural and tribal barriers. The call for a moratorium on foreign missionaries on the basis of the success of missions and the maturity of the church overseas is, therefore, invalid.

The Body Is One
Mission organizations should realize too that the body of Christ is international and interracial in nature. They should not discriminate as they often have on the basis of race or nationality. Instead of recruiting only whites from their own countries they should be open to all believers of like faith.

In Africa many criticize Christianity by saying that it is the white man's religion. The lily-white composition of most mission organizations does not help to dispel this idea at all. If anything it reinforces it.

White-only teams working in predominantly nonwhite situations are no longer satisfactory. Mission organizations should realize this and start to actively recruit among all races. Integrated teams working in harmony for their Lord at home and abroad will demonstrate the true nature of the body of Christ.

When I arrived in America I was very interested in finding out why black Christians did not feel constrained to go overseas with the gospel especially to their own motherland, Africa. Several black evangelical leaders told me that white

fellow Christians discouraged them from having interest in the
foreign field. Mrs. Ozzie Edwards of Michigan told me that
after graduating from Bible school she was very much interested in going to Africa as a missionary. She was told by white
Christians that she would not be welcomed by Africans who
would look down upon her because of her slave background.

There is also the case of Miss Mary Bethune, the highly
talented black woman who later founded a college and became
advisor to presidents. After graduating from Moody Bible
Institute she felt called to Africa as a missionary. Because of
her color, she could not find a mission board to accept her. Thus
Africa was deprived of her compassion and of her unique
abilities.[1]

In his book, *When God Was Black,* Bob Harrison tells of how
he was discriminated against by white, fellow evangelical
Christians. He writes,

A frequent rationalization (that) used to keep American
blacks out of Africa is that Africans do not want us there.
The argument went like this: If American Negroes went to
Africa they would like to live on the same standard of living
as any other missionary. The African wouldn't want that.
Since the Negro is black, they would expect him to live like
the black Africans.[2]

The conclusion was that it would be impossible for black Americans to have an effective ministry in Africa.

When Howard Jones, a black minister now a team member
of the Billy Graham Evangelistic Association, proposed to go to
Africa to preach, a white missionary lady from Africa discouraged him. She said,

Africans will not accept the Gospel from you as a Negro as
they accept it from us. You see, Africans would resent your
coming to tell them about Jesus Christ and their need of salvation because they consider themselves on the same plane
as yourself. They would expect you to dress, eat and live as
they do, and if you should refuse there would be offense. But

with the white missionary it is different because we are from another race and culture.[3]

I see no justification at all for assuming that Africans would expect black Americans to live as themselves. Africans are not children. They know that a good standard of living is not the prerogative of the white man only. Even within the African context itself there are many who through education and hard work have attained a standard of living comparable to those in many overseas countries including the United States. My own people would think I was crazy if after my many years of study I went back to live in a grass-thatched hut, hunting for my meat and plowing a few acres by ox plow for subsistence.

Robert Gordon tries to make a case for the continued segregation of mission societies.

This separate development has a sound sociological, anthropological rationale. This is true for missions as well as for the larger society. Missions are faced with a cultural distance between black and white personnel when they integrate their boards.

He then goes on to quote a leading evangelical professor of missions, Dr. Donald McGavran, who says,

Blacks, if they run their own program, could do an outstanding job.... Multi-racial teams will be riddled with cross-cultural adaptation problems. Until the brotherhood issue is solved in America, the separate groups should be kept in separate missions, with their own jurisdiction.[4]

This definitely does not reflect the body concept. Segregation of missions indeed may make a lot of psychological, sociological and anthropological sense. The only problem is that it also makes theological, biblical and spiritual nonsense.

Christ above Culture
If it is true that it is impossible for a black and a white brother to work side by side among Africans, Indians or Chinese, then we better stop singing "There is power in the blood." If the

power of the blood of the Lamb of God could cleanse vile sinners and make them with Christ joint heirs of the glories of heaven, then that blood has the power to help born again believers work together in love and unity despite the diversity of their cultural backgrounds. Christ is above culture and is able to make his servants transcend prejudice and bigotry.

In the New Testament God provided an example for the composition of missionary groups. Early missionary bands were multi-racial and multi-cultural.

Symeon, one of those who laid hands on Barnabas and Paul to send them as missionaries, was a black man (Acts 13:1). Paul was a Roman Jew from Tarsus in Cilicia (Acts 22:3). Barnabas was a Hellenistic Jew from the island of Cyprus (Acts 4:36). Luke was a Greek and former slave from Antioch. This is indicated by his name and profession of medicine. Timothy was of mixed parentage. His mother was a Jew and his father, a heathen Greek (Acts 16:1-3). Titus was an uncircumcised Greek (Gal. 2:3). Aristarchus was a native of Thessalonica. Tychicus and Trophimus were from Asia, which we know as Turkey today (Acts 20:4). They were from different racial and cultural backgrounds but were all one in Christ.

Christians tend to think that the early missionaries had no interpersonal, interracial or cross-cultural problems at all. This is a false picture. Paul and Barnabas had to part because of a serious interpersonal problem (Acts 15:36-39). Paul rebuked Peter strongly for apparent racism (Gal. 2:11-14). Paul was almost killed by racist Jews who accused him of bringing his Greek friends into the temple against established law (Acts 21:28). If he had thought on the same lines as Gordon and McGavran, he would have recruited only full blooded Jews as missionaries and urged Timothy and other non-Jewish Christians to form their own missionary bands.

To say that until the brotherhood question is settled in America missions should continue to segregate on grounds of color is to mislead. Christians should not follow the pattern set by secular culture. Unfortunately this has often been the case in America. Instead of giving the country much needed moral leadership, evangelical Christianity looks to secular culture to lead. The result is a national moral decline. A few small missions have always been open to all races. More need to follow their example. Some have taken a lead by changing their policies and welcoming applicants from all races in the United States and overseas countries as missionary candidates. The Africa Inland Mission publicly confessed their former discrimination against nonwhites and are now open to Christians of all races. They also took the bold step of bringing African missionaries from Kenya to work in some United States cities. The Evangelical Alliance Mission also opened their doors to other races. I was delighted one day to meet a black brother from Jamaica and a Philipino evangelist who are both going overseas as missionaries under TEAM.

Even though the situation is changing drastically in this respect, the problem is that blacks have been so turned off by their rejection in the past that they are no longer applying. Missions, therefore, have the responsibility to contact nonwhite churches in America and inform them of their openness so that those who may feel led into missionary work may consider applying to them. Missionary representatives also need to visit predominantly black Bible schools and colleges to give their presentations on missionary work and the opportunities for service which are available through their organizations.

It is hypocritical for mission boards to protest against a moratorium while they themselves are not open for all races to serve God within their organizations.

In his well-received paper at the International Congress on World Evangelization, Ralph Winter emphasized the importance of cross-cultural evangelism. He pointed out that four out of five non-Christians in the world today are beyond the reach of any Christians within their immediate geographical and cultural area. He also said that in Africa and Asia alone

there are two billion people without a witness. This means that
Christians still have to cross racial and cultural boundaries in
order to bring the message of salvation to these multitudes who
have not yet heard of the Savior.

Together We Learn

The importance of cross-cultural interaction, however, should
not be limited to evangelism but should be a permanent feature
of the life of the church of Jesus Christ on earth. Just as God
gives different gifts to individual members of the body, so also
he gives particular gifts to churches in all cultures for the edifi-
cation of the church worldwide. Christians in different areas of
the world need to open themselves to each other in sharing so
that they can be edified by their diverse but not divergent cultural gifts.

African and Oriental thought patterns are different from
Western thought patterns. Western man is dichotomistic and
his philosophical bent is pragmatic rationalism. His tools are
scientific empiricism. He wants to dissect, compartmentalize
and quantify things. His general outlook on life is from a
rational and individualistic perspective. Because of his psychological and cultural makeup, Western man has developed from
the Word of God a body of systematic theology which reflects
his background and is unique to himself.

The African is wholistic in his approach to life. He accepts a
whole without any desire to cut it up and peer at its insides to
see what makes it tick. To him the Trinity is not a challenge to
be understood and explained. It is accepted as fact because the
African admits that there are things on this earth which man
just does not have the capacity to understand, especially things
pertaining to God and the spirit world.

The African world is inhabited by both human and spiritual
beings. Demon activity, miracles and other nonempirical
phenomena pose no problems for him. These things which
bother the Western mind are as real to him as cells seen

through the microscope. The African is less interested in what a man believes and more interested in how he behaves. Social amenability is more emphasized than the correct comprehension of doctrine.

In the New Testament we read of our Lord going off into the mountain to pray all night. There is something cultural in that too, I believe. You see he was an Easterner, and Easterners are an introspective and meditative people.

At the Inter-Varsity Urbana Missionary Convention in 1973, I learned much from Phillip Teng of Hong Kong who gave the daily Bible exposition. Many of the salient points he brought out of the Scriptures could never have been brought out by an African or an American.

Books by Watchman Nee are very popular among evangelical Christians. I believe people read them because they have a perspective to the Word of God which is different. He describes the individual's relationship to God through the Holy Spirit in a way that makes you see it so clearly and you say, "Why did I not see that before?" You could not have seen that before unless you were an Oriental like him.

Our oneness in Christ should be visible in a respect for each other's cultures and in a willingness to accept and to learn from each other. By not being open to each other in our service for the Lord we deny ourselves many blessings.

It is imperative, therefore, that missionaries remove from their midst those things which cause national believers to call for a moratorium. The missionary's gifts should enhance and complement the gifts of those he ministers to, instead of retarding them. He should also be open to being ministered to by those he serves since they have a cultural perspective different from his own.

Moratorium Because of Frustration

4

The third group calling for a moratorium says that national churches can now do the work without external help. As I mentioned in chapter one, this has been overwhelmingly rejected by both missionaries and nationals, myself included. What is disturbing is that most of those who criticize this reason for a moratorium are not looking at all the arguments. They are quick to reject the idea as unscriptural and impractical, but they do not bother to go any deeper than that to analyze the motives of those who are calling for a moratorium. If we are to truly be one in Christ, we all need to be concerned about each other's concerns. If one part of the body hurts, the whole body is affected.

Not all the advocates of a moratorium base their case on anthropological reasons or on the success of missions. Some, like Gatu, call for a moratorium because of the frustration of working with missions which, instead of assisting national churches to grow, are now retarding their growth and maturing. This is a problem of where we should focus our efforts and not on whether the moratorium is spiritual or practical. Instead of just saying a moratorium is wrong, we should seriously work at getting rid of the cause of frustration.

Byang Kato is reported to have rejected the idea of a moratorium at the Lausanne Congress on World Evangelization. He is quoted as saying,

Gradual transfer of African leadership is our objective. The leading of the Spirit of God and the universality of the church are factors to be considered. A Kenyan may be called by the Spirit to serve in Latin America. A call for moratorium seems to be merely an emotional appeal without adequate consideration of the ramifications involved.[5]

I beg to differ slightly with Kato. Even though I, like him, reject the idea of a blanket moratorium, I do not see why transfer of church leadership from missionaries to nationals should be gradual. This is not the example set by Paul. As soon as he founded a church, he appointed local leaders to take over from him while he went to work elsewhere. In Africa we have missions which have been working in a particular country for fifty years or more. Up to now some of them have not transferred leadership to the nationals. This is unscriptural and is becoming more and more intolerable to national Christians.

It is true, as Kato says, that a missionary should be free to work anywhere in the world where the Spirit calls him. We in Africa need such called-ones to come and work with us. However, there should be a moratorium on those who are continuing to take positions which Africans should hold and on those who will come only to lead. We need men and women who will work within and under the authority of our local churches.

The Modern Missionary Pattern

The root of this problem lies in the history of the founding of our churches. Let me give a rough sketch of the pattern I have found from my experience in Rhodesia and from talking with Christians from other countries of the Third World.

When missionaries arrived in a new area, they established mission stations with schools and medical clinics. The first native converts who showed promise were given some Bible training and employed as evangelists at a salary by the missionaries. In the same way they employed teachers, nurses and maintenance workers. Teachers' salaries came from the government, but as school managers, missionaries had direct authority over school teachers. Most of the teachers were Christians, having graduated from mission schools.

Through much hard work on the part of both the missionary and the African evangelists, many churches were soon established all over the countryside. In order to cope with the growing number of churches, the missionary employed more evangelists and pastors.

A need grew for organization. The missionary was the final authority in the clinic, the school and the church. The African pastors and their elders were directly under him. He arranged the pastor's timetable. A church had nothing to say whatsoever about their pastor's conditions of employment or the amount of his salary.

In matters of church discipline it was the missionary who sat in judgment of erring national Christians. Sometimes the pastor and church elders would be brought in as advisors, but I have known cases where teachers were sacked from their positions without the church leaders being consulted because the missionary had heard from "reliable witnesses," that they were taking part in "immoral activities."

There was a marked employer/employee relationship between the missionary and the pastor. I have known of cases where, after every evangelistic trip, the pastor would be required by the mission to fill a form stating where he went, how many people he spoke to about salvation and how many were saved.

There is nothing inherently wrong with a pastor giving a report of his work to those he is responsible to. The issue in this case is that the pastor was reporting to the mission organization instead of to the elders and deacons of his church. In other words the pastor derived his leadership from the mission organization employing him and not from the congregation which he was pastoring.

In the late 1960s I observed an American missionary start a new work in Rhodesia. He first went to the government to ask for a piece of land on which to build a church even before he had any converts. When he was given the land, he engaged builders who put up a beautiful building, complete with spire and bell. This was paid for with money from his mission in the United States. After the church and the pastor's house were finished, he then started to invite people to the church and to preach to them. Among his first converts was a retired man who could read. He was immediately employed as the pastor of the church even though he had no formal Bible training. He was paid by the missionary who was regarded as the "great white father" who provides everything for the small congregation. If this is not ecclesiastical paternalism, then tell me what it is!

The Biblical Pattern
As one can see, this is a radical departure from the New Testament norm. In planting new churches most missionaries ignored the modes of evangelism used so successfully by Paul. He chose local leaders as soon as he founded a church, as we see in Acts 14:21-24. It is important to note that verse 23 says that Paul "committed them to the Lord in whom they believed." He left them to depend on the Holy Spirit. He did not set himself up as their leader and then gradually hand over leadership to them after many years of training as is the custom in modern-day missions.

Paul had virtually no control over the churches he founded. He had spiritual authority, but even when he heard of sin in the church, he pleaded with that church to discipline the erring brother in love, as we see in 1 Corinthians. He himself never sat in judgment of local Christians. This was the work of the church and not of the missionary. He assumed spiritual responsibility for them by agonizing over them in prayer, by exhorting and instructing them in the Word personally, by writing letters and by using counselors, like Timothy and Titus, whom he had trained. He never assumed direct administrative responsibilities over any church he founded.

In some missions African pastors were not permitted to perform marriages. They could not be ordained until after several years of service even though they had Bible school training. The term *reverend* was reserved for the white missionary only.

As the African became more sophisticated through education, international influence and study of the Bible, he started to question the validity of the mission's control of the church. Voices began to be raised in protest. The African churches asked to be masters of their own destiny under the authority of the Holy Spirit.

Instead of following New Testament principles and handing over control of the church to the nationals, most missions clung to power with the excuse that, "The African people are not ready to control the church yet." Protesting African Christians were labeled "troublemakers" and their motives were even brought to question.

Who Calls the Tune?

At this time many African Christians broke away to form their own churches which were immediately labeled *sects* by the missions. However, some of these so-called sects are doing a great work for God. They have a vitality and an evangelical zeal which is often lacking in many of the mission-related churches.

When African Christians persisted in their demand to control their churches, the missions reluctantly gave them a certain amount of authority. But they still could not do certain things without mission approval. They still had to follow various mission policies. They also could not amend their constitutions without mission approval.

When the church asked the missions to relinquish their control of the churches and the pastors, the missions agreed on the stipulation that the nationals now pay the pastors and finance their own programs. It was now a case of "He who pays the piper calls the tunes." Various missions formulated various schemes for phasing out of their financial commitments to the churches.

In the sending countries the word went out. The national churches were now becoming "indigenous." To many in the sending churches this sounded good and proper. What was not realized is that because the missionary had paid the pastors, built the churches and financed all the projects all along, the people had never been taught Christian stewardship. They still could see that the missionary was much richer than they were and therefore expected him to continue as general provider.

Others started to question their need for paid pastors. In many cases it was impractical for them to have one because the pastor's salary, which had come from the mission, was high above the earnings of the average tribesmen he ministered to. They would never be able to support him.

The missions persisted in their financial phase-out. Many pastors found themselves without support. One by one, some left their churches to earn a living elsewhere.

Many African churches have thus entered a time of crisis. Christians were not taught to witness. The pastor was doing all the work for them. Like the Western Christians, they were accustomed to coming to church on Sunday, hearing the sermon, going home and waiting for the next Sunday. The Western concept of a paid clergy, introduced by the missionaries, became a detriment to the natural growth of the African church.

Herbert Kane cites mission control of national churches and

the churches' desire to be independent as the main cause of church/mission tension today.

The most vexing of all problems is church-mission tension. The spirit of nationalism, running very strong in the Third World, has infected the churches. They have suddenly come of age and are demanding full autonomy. Some churches, of course, received their independence years ago before even the government got theirs. However, this was the exception, not the rule. Most missions dragged their feet, and when political independence came, neither they nor the churches were ready for it. Consequently tensions developed which have marred church-mission relations during the past decade. This is a problem that must be solved if the missions are to survive the decade of the seventies.[6]

Because this problem is largely not yet solved, many national Christian leaders are frustrated. They perceive the missions as unwilling to give them their independence and to assist them as equal brothers in Christ without paternalism.

Out of this milieu some are now saying the missionary should get out of the picture for a while (Gatu suggests five years) so that the churches can reorient themselves and organize to take up the slack that is there at present. They see missionary leadership as too distracting to the church for it to take its responsibilities seriously. They are not saying missionaries should stop reaching the unsaved but that they should stop controling the churches and the service ministries as many are at present doing.

Some missions claim that they have established independent churches when in fact those churches are not functionally independent. One such mission in Africa told the churches it had founded to organize themselves because the mission was now giving them their independence.

The churches organized themselves and formed an executive council. The council met to formulate a suitable form of church government. They decided to band together in a denomination with an episcopalian form of church government led by an elected bishop. They felt that this was quite in keeping with their culture and social temperament.

When the missionaries were told of these decisions, they were horrified. This was against their mission policy, they said. They insisted that each local church they had planted be autonomous according to their established policy.

After a protracted argument between the missionaries and the church leaders, the Africans relented and reluctantly agreed to compromise because the mission threatened to withdraw the funds it was giving to the church. This same mission seriously claims that they founded an independent, indigenous African church.

Supporting National Churches

Herbert Kane also cites the use of foreign funds as the stickiest of all problems on the mission field. He asks,

Can the churches on the mission field be truly self-governing if they are not fully self-supporting? Is it realistic to expect these churches, at this stage in their development, to assume full responsibility for all departments of the work? If foreign funds are used will there be any strings attached? Will the churches be expected to account to the missions for all foreign funds received and disbursed? Finally, will the supporting churches in the homeland be as keen to subsidize the overseas churches as they have been to support their own foreign missions?[7]

I was rather disappointed because Herbert Kane did not try to suggest some answers to these vexing questions from his own experience as a missionary overseas.

The biblical principle of establishing self-supporting churches is a sound one. As I have shown earlier, this principle was not followed. Foreign funds were used in establishing and maintaining national churches overseas. The result is that the American dollar crippled indigenous initiative and saddled the churches with expensive programs which they can never dream of financing themselves.

As members of one body Christians in the more affluent countries should indeed help their spiritual kin in poorer countries. When Judea was in the grip of famine, the churches of Antioch (Acts 11:29), Corinth and Galatia (1 Cor. 16:1-3) all gathered gifts which Paul carried to the believers in Jerusalem. God expects his children to be interdependent and to bear each other's burdens. However, this assistance did not carry with it the crippling paternalistic control which often follows some missionary largess today.

From their inception, national churches should be independent. The missionary should appoint elders for them as Paul did and leave the administration of the new church to them. His ministry should be that of a training teacher (2 Tim. 2:2). He should never employ and pay a pastor for them. If they feel they need a full-time pastor it is up to them to call one and to support him. They are the ones to engage a pastor and not the missionary.

If the missionary has funds that he would like to help the church with, he should give such funds to the whole church. Money should never be given as salary to individual evangelists or pastors. This only creates unfair patronage, favoritism and jealousy. If a pastor is employed, he should be employed by the church and be responsible to the church and not to the mission.

If funds from overseas are given to the church, the church leaders should determine how to use those funds according to their perceived needs. The missionary should feel free to advise on how best to use the funds, but he must never dictate how that money should be used. Since we assume that the money belongs to the Lord, the missionary should have the grace to accept the decision of the church even though he may feel that it could have been put to much better use. It is more important that the church maintain its independence and so learn by making mistakes. It is easier to learn to make sound decisions by actually making decisions than by someone making the decisions for you.

After giving money to a national church, some missions insist that they determine how that money should be used. They say that because God entrusted that money to them, it is their duty as good stewards to see that the Lord's money is used wisely. Of course to them the wise way to use the money is what they themselves perceived to be wise. Because of this kind of attitude, people like Gatu are calling for a moratorium on missionary money and personnel. They are tired of being treated like children.

It should also be pointed out that the majority of missions do not teach national believers to be self-sufficient by showing them ways of getting into the mainstream of economic life and thus generating resources for their own churches. Financing national work with national resources is the subject of the next chapter.

The Place of
Service Ministries
5

Another major source of church/mission conflict is the place of service ministries. In countries where indigenous people have assumed responsibilities in all areas of life, missionary work often sticks out like a sore thumb because of its foreign nature. Service ministries like radio, literature, Bible schools, hospitals and clinics are still firmly in the hands of Western missionaries. In many cases they are just as foreign as the American embassy, though one or two national leaders may sit on the governing boards or committees.

The lack of indigenous leadership is used by critics to point to Christianity as the white man's religion. They accuse national Christians of being the lackeys of the Americans and British who direct the work and tell them what to do.

Because of the growing sense of nationalism fostered by political independence from colonial governments, nationals started to ask not only for the control of their churches but also of the service ministries started by the missions. Some missions handed over control of the church to nationals but were reluctant to hand over the leadership of service ministries. One reason, which seems legitimate enough, is that standards may fall and general inefficiency if not total breakdown will be the result. But the root of the problem does not lie with the nationals but with the missionaries who did not have the foresight to strategically train the nationals at the highest level for responsible leadership. (I will discuss higher education for nationals specifically in the next chapter.)

A few missions have done a commendable job in training and introducing Africans into these ministries. An example is the Sudan Interior Mission work in Nigeria. Most of their radio, literature and Bible school work is steadily being taken over by well-trained nationals. They have a scholarship program which is helping prepare national leaders by giving them training overseas which they cannot get at home.

Even in these few cases, however, it was often pressure from national governments which compelled the missions to train and place Africans in responsible positions. They insisted that all agencies be controlled by nationals. I have observed that the trend toward the Africanization of ministries is most evident in independent African countries. In the countries of southern Africa where white governments are still in control, missionaries do not seem to be in any hurry to train nationals to take over from them.

What is most distressing to me is to see missionaries retiring and instead of their positions being filled by nationals, their children have been coming back as missionaries to take over from them. They in turn become our new bookstore managers, directors of ministries and hospital administrators. They are actually making dynasties out of their missionary kingdoms in our countries. In such cases is the call for a moratorium not legitimate?

The Director Syndrome

I have observed among evangelical missionaries what I call

The Director Syndrome. It seems as though a good number of missionaries do not feel their ministry is important unless they are director of something. There is, therefore, much unholy jostling for positions of leadership among them. The result is that qualified nationals are not even considered for positions they could possibly fill. I know of bookstore managers, Bible correspondence school directors and other missionaries who hold positions which could be filled by nationals.

In order to justify this perpetuation of the status quo, some missionaries have created and communicated to churches overseas an unflattering and negatively stereotyped image of the African. He is cast as eternally inefficient. We, therefore, hear things like, "The Africans are not trained enough. The whole idea of a simple business transaction is foreign to them. They are not like us." I have often been amazed to hear such sentiments voiced by missionaries working in areas of Africa where some of the continent's most sophisticated and articulate people are to be found.

The missionary presentations I saw in America also left much to be desired. They only highlighted what Western missionaries were doing for various peoples of the Third World. There was too little mention of the nationals' contribution as witnesses among their own people or even as ministers to the missionaries' own needs. In the missionary periodicals and bulletins the role of the national was almost always depicted as that of recipient or assistant, rarely that of coworker. This stereotype also includes dishonesty. I have personally heard missionaries say, "We don't entrust large sums of money to the nationals because you cannot even trust the Christians. They will use it on themselves."

Sometimes national churches will want to carry out certain projects that seem important to them. When they approach the mission with a request for funds, they may not get the money unless the mission sees the project as being important. One day I was in a meeting where funds were being discussed. One missionary said, "We missionaries are entrusted with the Lord's money as stewards. We must, therefore, make sure that these funds are not squandered carelessly."

The problem with this attitude is that stewardship is no longer viewed as the responsibility of all the saints. It is removed from being a spiritual quality to a racial or ethnic quality. Thus only North American missionaries qualify to be stewards.

Many Africans do not see any possibility of becoming the administrators, school principals, treasurers and decision makers of mission ministries. Instead they see more and more missionaries coming to do work that they rightly feel they should be doing. Is it any wonder then that they are calling for a halt to the influx of more missionaries?

Pragmatic national leaders, especially those under mission employ, strongly disagree with the idea of a moratorium. They know that American churches give to individual missionaries and not to the work in general. They consider the ramifications involved in a moratorium and realize that if the missionary goes, the money goes with him. They, therefore, prudently criticize a moratorium as impractical and unscriptural. But they fail to touch on what gave rise to the issue.

I strongly feel that there should be no restriction put on any servant of God who wants to come to Africa to proclaim the good news of salvation to those who have not heard and to persuade those who have heard to accept Christ as Savior. However, I feel equally strongly that all restrictions should be put on missionaries coming to Africa to do work which can be done by Africans. We need only those missionaries who are qualified and willing to train Africans for responsibility. There is no longer room for missionaries who will come to work as directors without Timothys at their side who will eventually take over from them. Such missionaries will never be out of work because Africa has millions of Timothys waiting to be trained in order to train others.

"We Have Done Everything"

Some missionaries are shocked and perplexed when confronted by ungrateful attitudes and even open hostility from nationals. They wring their hands in agony and say, "What have we done wrong? We have done everything for these people, but they actually resent us." They fail to see that their mistake *was* that they did everything for the national. They successfully took away his pride in their zeal to help.

The African needed a hospital, so they built one for him. It never crossed their mind to protect his pride by building the hospital with him and consulting him. The church needed a Bible school, so the missionaries raised money from the States and built a beautiful school for them. They named it after the American family which gave the largest sum. Again they did not consult the Africans. They fail to understand why the Africans do not call the school by the official name given by the mission. They prefer to call it by the African name of the hill upon which it is built. The mission also decided to start a litera-ture committee and started to employ workers. No national was on the committee.

African Christians have no pride in most of these ministries. They had nothing to do with their inception and have little or nothing to do with how they are run. They belong to the mis-sionaries who organized and who run them. Africans only re-ceive the services rendered and are expected to say, "Thank you."

The problem with a good number of missions is that they think they know what the national needs without even asking him. Sometimes this assumption can bear painful results.

In 1970 a certain mission decided that the church needed a theological-education-by-extension program. The conference, composed solely of missionaries, appointed a missionary couple to establish the program and prepare the lesson materials. For a whole year this couple worked hard. They wrote lessons which were translated into the national language by national workers. Finally the materials were mimeographed and the program was ready to go.

It was only after everything was done that the national church conference was officially informed of this program which was supposed to help their church. The mission asked the church for pastors who would work with the missionary couple in putting the program to work. The church leaders politely but firmly refused to have anything to do with the program. They had their own programs to attend to.

If this mission had presented the idea to the church in the beginning and asked them whether they felt it was needed or not, a lot of unhappiness and unfortunate waste could have been avoided. The last I heard was that the mission decided to employ a national Christian to work with the missionaries on it. In a confrontation between church and mission, the mission usually has its way because it supplies the funds for much of the work.

In another instance the missionaries were very enthusiastic about the success of Evangelism-in-Depth campaign in Latin America and West Africa. "This is what our African church needs," they concluded. Immediately they started to work out the details for its implementation. In the words of the missionaries concerned, "No effort was spared to make it complete and workable."

When the program was presented to the church conference, replete with well-prepared booklets and tracts, the church leaders politely endorsed it but never put it into effect. They were actually not interested in it in the least. Of course the missionaries spiritualized this failure away by saying, "It was a good program, but it wasn't God's time for it." They failed to see that if they had involved the national leadership from the very beginning, the program would probably have succeeded. If they had consulted the church first, a lot of waste could have been avoided.

In America I noticed that everybody has a fierce sense of

independence and a revulsion to receiving any charity. Even students are proud if they are paying their own way through college. Some look down on students who depend on their parents for everything. Africans are not very much different. They appreciate a hand when they are in need but resent being made perpetual beggars, which is what missions have made them into. They want to help themselves. Surely this is not too much to ask.

What Are the Solutions?

Herbert Kane wonders if it is realistic to ask national churches at this stage in their development to assume full responsibility for all departments of their work.[8] My answer is an emphatic No! National churches cannot support all departments of their work because the missions attached expensive ministries like hospital work, publishing and broadcasting which can never be funded from their meager church collections.

I am not saying these ministries should not have been started. They are, in fact, needed for evangelism. Can you imagine Christian work in Africa without the ministries of radio, literature, hospitals and training schools? I am only opposed to a structure which ties them to churches which have only a limited amount of support. These parachurch ministries should be organizationally divorced from the churches which they serve and be established as independent, nonprofit organizations under the directorship of boards of trustees.

In America most Christian literature comes from independent publishing houses run by laymen, like David C. Cook and Scripture Press. Evangelical Christian schools, like Dallas, Wheaton, Moody, Fuller and Gordon Conwell, are also independent of churches. They are run by educators who are dedicated to serving the churches by training Christian men and women. The same model of private enterprise can be seen in the organization of Christian radio stations and studios, film producers and TV stations.

This is not happening overseas. Those few missions which are handing over responsibilities to nationals are handing over to the national churches responsibilities for all the ministries too. We therefore have bishops and general secretaries of churches struggling with the burden of administering over one hundred and some churches, two or more hospitals, a recording studio, three Bible schools, a scholarship program and a growing publishing work. The result of this kind of transfer is that it perpetuates dependence on the mission and does not encourage excellence in production.

How does this happen? To prepare the national church leader to run the empire the mission has placed on his shoulders, he usually has only three years of Bible school training after his primary education. In rare cases he may have a B.A. in Bible from England or the United States. This does not help him much in his demanding task. The result is that he is often only a figurehead. The missionaries continue to make the decisions as before and continue to fund the ministries with money from overseas.

Thus in most evangelical parachurch ministries, salaries of both missionaries and nationals come from overseas. All other expenses are paid for with money raised out of the country. If the missions were compelled by circumstances to leave, the ministries would not be able to survive for a day. They would collapse because of lack of funds even though the nationals might have the technical know-how to run them.

Commenting on this problem James Johnson, Executive Director of Evangelical Literature Overseas, said,

> It is a much discussed fact inside national "Understudies" circles in communications centers overseas that if the national had to take over tomorrow from the missionary radio station or publishing house, that at least eight out of ten would go defunct. The national has not been taught, nor are his chances for education very hopeful on how to make his station or publishing house run on commercial levels. With-

out American church financial support as subsidy, there is no way for a purely national communications program to survive except by going commercial. For many "national leaders" the future offers some grim hand-writing on the wall.[9]

If the missions had assisted trustworthy nationals to set up the publishing ministries as self-supporting businesses, it would make no difference if the missions left. It would free church leaders trained in theology and pastoral work to be totally involved in the work of church administration, prayer, counseling, preaching and teaching without being encumbered with the complex administration of empires of churches, bookstores, hospitals, schools, radio and publishing houses.

This would also improve the quality of materials being produced. Often mission literature is inferior in quality because the producers have no incentive to do better. Their literature is sold cheaply or given away free. They don't have to sell it to make a profit since their income is guaranteed by the mission in America.

If they were making their living from that ministry, like other publishing ministries in the United States, they would be forced to produce superior quality material because it would have to compete with others on the market place. Often the mission publisher is sincere. He really wants to come up with a better product, but because he is not in the money market, he has no way of knowing whether his product is good or not.

I have often heard missionaries say that missions have to subsidize the literature they produce because Africans cannot afford to pay much for books. I totally disagree with the premise. If secular publishing houses are selling books at competitive prices to Africans, a Christian publisher can do the same. Africans will buy books if they meet a felt need. Educational authorities found some of the books I wrote in my language to be suitable for use as supplementary readers in the public schools. These are books which clearly show the way of salvation. I am sure that in many countries of the Third World Christian publishing businesses run by nationals can succeed. However, African laymen need help with capital and proper training in business methods.

Along with making parachurch ministries self-supporting Western churchmen with capital could do much by assisting their Third World brothers and sisters in developing and utilizing local resources which in many cases they have in abundance. Instead of Christian businessmen coming to our countries only to invest for their own profit, they could assist national Christians with capital and know-how so that they would be in a position to support their own ministries just as American businessmen support missions and other ministries at home.

Here is an illustration of what can be done. After studying in the United States a young African Christian was helped with some money by a missionary friend. He added to it by borrowing from other friends. The missionary then helped him to negotiate a franchise there with Service Master. After some time he wrote Service Master in the United States asking them to decide what he should do with their share of the profits since the government would not allow him to send the money out of the country. Service Master in the United States, who themselves contribute to Christian work, advised him to give the money and all future profits to Christian work in the country. If this story could be repeated again and again, after a number of years we would not need a penny from overseas for the support of our work in Africa. We might even start to support nationals going overseas as missionaries.

In many of the faith missions individual missionaries raise money in their home countries for their own support and the support of their own ministry. When a national takes over the work, the missionary takes the support with him, leaving the national without the much-needed financial base.

While studying in the United States I met a young African

man who was obviously overworked. He explained to me that he was trying to earn a degree while at the same time raising funds for his future ministry. He said that he had worked in this ministry with the missionary founder for many years. He was sent to the United States to study in order to take over the leadership of the ministry from the missionary who was going to start a different work.

The missionary had raised all the money for the ministry, and he was taking this support to the new ministry. So the young man was asked to raise his own support and the support for the new ministry while studying in the United States. Because of a heavy study schedule and lack of contacts, the young man was not able to raise any money in American churches. They were not used to the idea of supporting nationals directly. In many cases they were not aware of the poor financial condition of overseas Christians, and they therefore felt that national workers should be supported by their own people.

Because the young man could not raise money for his family's support and the support of his ministry, he became frustrated. He told me that he was seriously considering giving up this Christian work. He felt that he would be better off working for some commercial company in his country.

Because of this mode of support, many faith missions are reluctant to put trained nationals in responsible positions. They have no money to pay adequate salaries. They would rather keep the ministries in the hands of missionaries who raise the funds for them. If they do employ a national, he is usually paid a much lower salary than that of the missionary even though he may have the same education and training. Because of this, many well-trained nationals are not willing to work full-time in faith-mission ministries.

If businessmen were helping national Christians to develop support, as did Service Master, problems like this could be solved. Many service ministries would feel freer to put nationals in positions of leadership.

Training Nationals for Leadership

6

I have discussed some of the problems associated with failure to train and to turn over responsibilities to nationals. Here I will look more closely at what training is needed, how it should be carried out and what its implications will be for the body of Christ in the Third World.

Bible School Training

Most missions establish Bible schools to train prospective clergy and to give a good biblical background to laymen. They are generally patterned after Bible schools in America which concentrate only on teaching the Bible and related subjects.

The first Bible school graduates were employed as pastors or workers in the different mission ministries. As more and more graduated from the Bible schools, more of the pastorates and mission jobs were filled. The result is that we now have many trained young people from Bible schools who are unemployed. Unlike the well-to-do churches of America, African churches do not have such positions as assistant pastor, youth minister,

minister of music, minister of Christian education and so on.

The stated goal of these Bible schools is to train Christians so that they can go back into their communities to be witnesses for Christ. However, the present curriculum of most of them does not equip nationals to be productive and respected members of their societies.

Some young people with Bible school diplomas now feel their training was a waste of time and money. Because they could not get mission jobs, they feel cheated. Their diplomas do not help them to secure jobs or to be helpful and needed members of their communities because they only studied the Bible.

If Bible schools are going to be relevant, they should incorporate curriculum which meets the felt needs of the people. They must, along with biblical subjects, teach trades like agriculture, bricklaying, livestock raising, welding, well digging as well as business and commercial courses. With such training Christian nationals will be able to move into the mainstream of the economic life of their developing nations and be respected members of their communities. Success will be reflected in their giving to churches, thus lessening dependence on foreign funds.

Unfortunately when some missionaries are asked by nationals to include this kind of training in the Bible schools, the reply is, "We did not come here to be involved in social work. There are others who can do that. Our duty is to teach the Word of God." If Bible schools will continue to use teaching programs imported from overseas without structuring them to meet local needs, they will have problems with both national Christian leaders and governments in the future.

One day I talked to an angry African Christian leader. As a principal of a Bible school in Africa, he saw the need to provide protein for his students. He bought some chickens which the students were happy to take care of. They multiplied and soon the school had a steady supply of eggs. The hope was that some day the chickens would provide meat for the dining table too.

When he went on a study leave, an American missionary took over as principal. He promptly sold all the chickens. To him it was ludicrous for a Bible school to raise chickens. To the nationals the chicken project was a significant step toward self-sufficiency.

In another part of Africa people were compelled to sell their cattle in an effort to rid the area of the tsetse fly. When the tribesmen sold all their cattle, they had much money but nothing to pull their plows with. Families combined their money and bought tractors from the city.

The first year people were very happy because the tractors enabled them to plow more land than usual. Those without tractors rented them from their neighbors. The second year was different. Some of the tractors started to have problems.

At a mission station in the middle of this district was a missionary with unusual mechanical abilities. The farmers soon started to knock on his door, asking him to fix their tractors. He obliged and would go to see what was wrong.

He was amazed because sometimes he was called for very elementary problems like changing spark plugs, oil or cleaning the carburetor. He concluded that what these people needed was training in simple mechanics. He therefore approached his mission with the proposal that he be allowed to start a school giving training in Bible and mechanics. His proposal apparently was not taken seriously by the mission for the school never materialized. After he left, many of the people in the area lost their tractors because they could not repair them and the town was too far away for them to get the help they needed.

Fortunately more and more mission leaders are getting away from a narrow concept of mission and of their task as Bible teachers. In his book *Third World and Mission*, Dennis Clark says,

> Christian training, therefore, must not be so highly concentrated on sophisticated theological concepts as to neglect a Bible training for the pastors, teachers, and evangelists who

will serve rural communities. This training needs to relate the Bible to life, to provide courses for farmers and their wives with advice on family planning, digging wells, increasing wheat and rice yield, exterminating pests, digging latrines, and other practical problems. Such a package training would be far more valuable than two or three years of Greek.[10]
A creative Bible school incorporating trade subjects could be self-supporting. Students could grow their own food, make their own furniture and even put up some of the school buildings. Some of the school produce could be sold for income for the school.

Graduate Level Training
In an article on the future of foreign missions (*Eternity,* February 1972), Eric Fife mentions higher education for nationals as an area that needs attention. He says, "Missions have always done a superb work in establishing primary and secondary schools. However, the record at higher levels has been poor." As an African Christian I not only endorse Fife's observations, but I say that higher education should be the priority for many missions today and not just another area needing attention.

In Africa there are two areas which urgently need trained, national leadership. These are theology and communications —the content and the means to propagate it.

There is an urgent need for theological training at a higher level because the church is facing challenges threatening its very life. These challenges can best be met by well-trained African theologians. Dr. John Mbiti, an African scholar and theologian himself, wrote,

The missionaries who began this modern phase of Christian expansion in Africa, together with their African helpers, were devout, sincere and dedicated men and women. But they were not theologians, some of them had little education,

and most of the African evangelists and catechists were either illiterate or had only little formal learning. These workers were more concerned with practical evangelism, education and medical care, than with any academic or theological issues that might arise from the presence of Christianity in Africa. Mission Christianity was not, from the start, prepared to face a serious encounter with either the traditional religions and philosophy or the modern changes taking place in Africa. The church here now finds itself in the situation of trying to exist without a theology.[11]
Because of the lack of trained clergy, many of the young people pouring out of African high schools and universities look down upon the church. Our poorly trained pastors are finding it harder and harder to minister, especially in the urban centers. They are struggling to minister effectively to congregations with growing numbers of government officials, lawyers, doctors, nurses, policemen, clerks, teachers and professionals of all kinds with overseas training when they themselves have had little academic and theological education.

Although the African church is growing by leaps and bounds, its spiritual depth is shallow in some cases and the quality of its life far from robust. This lack of depth can be attributed to the absence of an indigenous theology. What little theology there is, is Western theology super-imposed on the African church without systematic or deliberate adaptation to the culture of the people. Because of this, the questions African Christians are facing remain unanswered, questions having to do with family life and their relationship to traditional customs, rites and festivals which are part of their culture.

In Nigeria some evangelical Christians found themselves in serious conflict with the rest of the community. The village had a "talking drum" which was the symbol of their unity. Whenever there was something of great importance, the elders of the village broadcast it over this drum to everybody.

After this drum was old and damaged the village decided to

make a new one. The making of a new tribal drum is something of major significance in which all adults of the village are expected to participate by contributing money and food for the festival that goes with it. Everybody was involved in preparing for this important occasion in the life of the village. The Christians were conspicuous by their absence.

When the elders of the village asked them why they were not taking part, they said they were Christians and, therefore, would not participate in such heathen activities. This infuriated the elders who saw it, primarily, as a lack of patriotism and a rejection of the village authority. They demanded that Christians be ostracized since they thought themselves better than everybody else in the village.

The Christians saw themselves as faithful believers being persecuted for their faith. They received much encouragement from the missionaries who admired them for "standing up against heathen worship." The conflict between the Christians and the rest of the village was, therefore, heightened. Whereas before the village elders had respected the Christians and left them alone, they now saw them as a threat to their authority and to the unity of the village.

If someone had made a study of the religious, social and political significance of the talking drum, he would have been able to advise the Christians in a way that would have minimized conflict with their village.

In the making of a new talking drum there is one main thing which Christians could not participate in. This is the sacrifice of a chicken to dedicate and purify the drum. The Christians could have participated in all the festival with a clear conscience. When it came time to sacrifice the chicken, they could have respectfully asked to be excused. They could also have used it as a time for witness. Since their sacrifice was Christ who died on the cross, all creation is pure, including the talking drum, and does not need the blood of a chicken to purify it. In this way they would not have been perceived as challenging the very leadership of the village. They would have addressed themselves to a theological issue without undermining the whole institution of the talking drum.

In America on the Fourth of July people in large and small cities have parades. As the parade comes people lining the sides of the streets take off their hats and put their right hand over their hearts in respect to the American flag which will be held by soldiers leading the procession. Both Christians and non-Christians respect the flag. In fact, the flag is so highly esteemed that in many churches you can find one beside the pulpit.

In Nigeria the talking drum has as much significance as Old Glory has to Americans. Dishonoring the flag is perceived by many as a serious act of insubordination. It is the same in Nigeria. Refusing to honor the talking drum is a serious act of insubordination to the village of which one is a member.

Africa needs a theology which deals with theological questions like this one which are peculiar to Africa. Foreign missionaries cannot produce such a theology. Africa's own sons need to be trained so that they in turn will be used by the Holy Spirit to teach a pure doctrine within the context of their culture and world view. Only thus can the church have a truly African theology.

In the past educated Africans did not want to identify openly with African religion because they would be regarded as ignorant and superstitious. Today the picture has changed. The rise of nationalism has made the African take pride in his cultural heritage. We therefore now have university graduates and teachers who are spirit mediums. Educated people now consult witch doctors and wear fetishes openly.

Some are rejecting Christianity as the white man's religion. They are talking of articulating African religions by giving them their own literatures. Some African political leaders encourage this type of thinking. They see this as a way of bringing unity to their young nations.

Evangelical Christianity is indeed not prepared for such a serious encounter with traditional African religions. When I was in Bible school, we learned about many non-Christian religions including some which did not exist to any extent in Africa. However, we did not study the religion of our own people because our missionary teachers did not know anything about ancestor worship. Up to now there is very little study and research into this by Christians. Much of the study has been done by humanist anthropologists who, in many cases, take a dim view of missions.

Because of their ignorance, missionaries have sometimes offended even some Christians by their total condemnation of African religion. They see traditional religion as only evil and satanic, and fail to appreciate the positive elements in its philosophy. They could treat this religion with respect and still produce a cogent apologetic for Christianity as the "power of God unto salvation." African Christians are not equal to this task now because they lack higher theological training. Only Africans trained at the highest level and able to work from the original language of the Bible will be able to give the church an apologetic which will demonstrate the veracity of Christianity in African terms.

Almost all African universities have departments of religion and philosophy. Most of them have no evangelical influence and therefore teach liberal and even syncretistic theology that denies the fundamental teachings of the Bible.

Noting this trend, Byang Kato made some very pertinent observations: In the March 10, 1973, issue of *Christianity Today* he is quoted as saying, "The Spiritual battle for Africa this decade will largely be fought on theological grounds. I have personally been challenged by the fact that most theological writing at a scholastic level, is by liberals or those sympathetic to liberal theology."

The lack of African evangelical scholarship is a direct result of the anti-intellectual inclination of evangelicals. This in-

clination grew as a reaction to rationalistic scholasticism of the
seventeenth and eighteenth centuries which denied the complete authority of the Scriptures. Many evangelicals seem to
feel that scholarship automatically leads to theological liberalism. This of course is not true. Christianity is actually a marriage of scholarship and piety as it has been throughout its two
thousand year history.

If the lack of evangelical scholarship is not remedied, the
church in Africa is going to be ill equipped to survive the next
decade. It is facing questions vital to its health which very few
are qualified to answer. It is faced with serious problems that
require not pat answers with Bible verses to match but serious
study and thought.

Some of these problems have to do with the relationship of
African Christians to traditional customs, festivals and rites
which are part and parcel of their culture. Others have to do
with theological issues peculiar to Africa. Much of the present
rhetoric on these subjects comes from liberal black pens. Where
are the fast growing evangelical churches going to find guid-
ance? If there is no emergence of evangelical scholars who will
grapple with these issues and produce a meaningful and cogent
systematic theology, the church will continue to become more
and more irrelevant.

Kato sees higher theological training for African evangelical leaders as the only way to meet, head on, the challenge of
liberalism and syncretism which is emerging. But it is not only
a necessity because of these challenges. Africa also needs to be
heard beyond her borders.

Ancient Africa contributed much to world theological
thought through the writings of men like Augustine and Ter-
tullian. Modern Africa has yet to add her voice to the contem-
porary theological scene which in many ways is still in the mire
of rational cynicism. Maybe, through a fresh and vibrant
African theology, the Christian world could experience a much
needed revival.

Communications Training

The world communications boom has made a tremendous impact on Africa. Missions and churches are well aware of the importance of the mass media in both the proclaiming of the gospel and the making of disciples. Almost every mission has some kind of a literature or radio ministry. However, I still see the trend among evangelicals as that of recruiting Western missionaries to come and do the work. Very few are training nationals at a level where they will eventually be able to run their own radio and literature ministries.

In Africa there is an urgent need to train nationals to use the media of literature and radio because these are the key media which are now well established across the continent.

1. *Literature.* Much of the Christian literature in Africa was written by missionaries. Some of it was written or translated from English by Africans who had rather limited training. Most of it is elementary and deals with such mundane subjects as smoking, drinking, dancing and the evils of having more than one wife.

In order for the African church to really mature, a robust Christian literature must come from the pens of committed, well-trained African writers dealing with the deeper implications of Christianity in African life. Unfortunately we have too many people who are eager to use literature in Africa that proved successful overseas—from *Pilgrim's Progress* to "The Four Spiritual Laws"—without regard to its relevancy to the African situation.

One day I saw two African girls reading a book on courtship and marriage in a Bible school library in Africa. As they read they giggled and nodded their heads in agreement with what the book was saying. This worried me because I had read the book which was published in America.

I was concerned because, among other things, the book said a girl should date several boys before she decides on marrying one. If our Christian girls would practice that, they would be regarded as very immoral by our society. Dating, American style, is not our custom.

Only African Christians can write books for our young people on courtship and marriage which also take into account the social change that we are undergoing due to Western influences without outraging our traditional customs. Unfortunately we have too many missionaries who insist on writing Christian literature for Africans. Some missionaries today, instead of training nationals in creative writing, do the writing themselves and then ask the nationals to translate.

There are very few missionaries who can write in the idiom of the people and at the same time meet a real need with their literature. A few have managed to do so in English. One such is Walter Trobisch who has written several booklets on African courtship and marriage. I should, however, point out that his popularity may also be due to the fact that there are almost no Africans as academically qualified as he is who are writing at the same level.

Africa Christian Press, based in Ghana, is doing much to inspire and encourage new authors. A good number of their titles are meeting real needs and answering questions young Africans are asking. But even with them I can guess that their greatest need is for authors who are trained and disciplined to write meaningful Christian literature. They cannot find enough writers for the books they would like to publish.

Africa has a growing secular literature from the pens of African intellectuals which is gaining respect at home and a place among the literature of the world. The sad thing is that much of it is largely critical of missions and Christianity. Many writers equate Christianity with colonialism and neocolonialism.

My own literary hero, Ezekiel Mphahlele, a man whom I have adored since I started to appreciate literature, is one of these writers. He artfully expresses with accuracy what I as an African would like to say to the world. This man is admired and emulated by many young African intellectuals. I was shocked to read in a bulletin from the University of Texas that he had said that Africans, to be truly free, must give up Christianity. He said, "When we have eventually diverted ourselves completely of the Christian myth we will know we have won a battle."[12]

African Christians writing at the same level as Mphahlele are conspicuous by their absence in Africa. We desperately need authors who will be recognized nationally and internationally for their literary prowess and at the same time stand tall for Christ and his Kingdom.

2. *Radio*.   Most Africans can now afford transistor radios. Many of them are being assembled in Africa and are inexpensive. All one has to do, if he lives in the village, is to sell one or two of his goats, and he will have the price of a transistor radio. He may also need to sell a chicken for the batteries. On many grass-thatched African roofs today are one or two reeds joined together as antennae for transistor radios.

In some of the remote and traditional areas of Africa, people literally live in their fields to protect their crop from wild animals. They build tree lookouts where someone sits day and night to protect their produce. They have with them a gong or drum which they beat to chase away baboons, buffaloes, elephants and other animals that may come to feed on their precious plants.

If we go together to Africa, we will probably see a man sitting on such a lookout platform. Next to his drum or gong we will also see a transistor radio. If we ask him to come down, he will graciously oblige. This man, who has never been to school a day in his life, who has never been outside his immediate area and who has never put a pair of shoes on his feet, will come down. He will come down and discuss with us the latest international news.

Fantastic! you say. So it is. The news comes to him translated into his own language. He and many other uneducated tribesmen are as well informed of world events as any sophisticated metropolitan.

The big question is, Who is doing the informing? In many cases unscrupulous people seeking to further their own ends realize the power of radio and use it effectively to communicate to the masses of Africa. Unfortunately Christians are not utilizing the media of radio for Christ as well as they could. Much is being done by several missions and organizations, but the training of nationals is still negligible.

A few years ago a certain mission built a well-equipped radio studio. The missionary director of the studio worked with a number of nationals in producing plays which were broadcast through the government operated national network.

People responded positively to the programs. Many were finding Christ through them. The director of broadcasting of the government network wrote the studio a letter of commendation and encouragement. He mentioned that he appreciated the high moral tone of the programs.

After a year the missionary, who alone could operate the recording console, had to come to America on furlough. Because there was no missionary to take over from him, the studio was closed and the work came to a stop. None of the Africans were trained to operate the console even though they could write scripts and dramatize the plays. Even today no nationals are being trained so as to continue that work. Instead that mission is now advertising in America for a missionary to go and direct the work of that studio.

Is it surprising then that nationals are calling for a moratorium on missionaries? As long as more missionaries come they do not see any chance for themselves to be real leaders. They see their future as that of perpetual assistants.

National Leadership
Most African governments are looking for communications experts. Many of them are employing expatriates who cost them

much money. Missions have the unique opportunity of strategically training Christian men and women who could fill important positions in their countries. The repercussions of such a strategy could be far-reaching.

These Christian communicators could provide much needed leadership to their nations. As gatekeepers of information flow they would be instrumental in steering their countries toward moral and godly ideologies, thus creating situations in which the gospel can be preached without hindrance.

It is unfortunate that some missions discouraged national Christians from taking part in politics. Many felt that it was wrong for Africans to fight British or French colonialism. They supported imperialism just as some missions support white supremacy in southern Africa today. If they had not discouraged so many, maybe we would have more African Christians in politics than we have today.

Well-qualified Christians are desperately needed in politics. With Christian leadership, African nations will adopt political and social systems which are basically ethical and which reflect a belief in God by their respect for human dignity.

Christian Colleges

The only way higher education could be made available is through the establishment in Africa of degree-granting Christian colleges which could turn out not only church leaders but leaders in all the areas of society. The impact of Christian colleges on American society has been great. The large missionary army that has left the shores of the United States to serve overseas is one evidence of that impact. The United States has over eight hundred Christian colleges. Africa, with over three times the land area and over one and one-half times the population of the United States, does not have one degree granting Christian college except Sudan Interior Mission's Igbaja Seminary in Nigeria, which gives a B.A. in theology. Evangelical churches and missions need to cooperate in building Christian colleges of higher learning for the church of Africa which by the year 2000 may very well be the largest church in the world. Since Christian training at higher levels is not available in Africa at present, deserving nationals should also be assisted to study abroad. This is the subject of the next chapter.

Sponsoring Nationals for Overseas Study

7

My interest in sponsoring nationals to study overseas was first aroused by an article I read in the October 1971 issue of *The Fields,* an evangelical missionary magazine. In it William MacDonald discusses things which hinder missionary work overseas. Among others, he cites the sponsorship of students from Third World countries for study in the United States as one of these.

Young people from many of the poorer countries of the world have an enormous desire to come to this country for education—high school, college, any kind of education, just to leave their own country for the land flowing with milk and honey! Their initial contact is often made with Americans on religious tours, or by mail. By deft diplomacy they obtain funds for the trip and sponsorship in the United States.

Once they are here it is understandable if they become intoxicated with the materialism of our affluent society. Their spiritual vitality takes a nose dive. They lose any desire to go back to serve the Lord in their own country.

Of course, sometimes they are forced to return by immigration laws. Often they go back with a reluctant heart, and with little zeal for Christian service among their own people. They have lost the common touch anyway; culturally and economically they are now upper class. And they impatiently wait a call to take back the Gospel to America.

MacDonald is to be commended for raising the subject which unfortunately has not been given the prominence it deserves in Christian circles. It is regrettable, however, that he writes in a sarcastic style which is rather simplistic in its generalizations. He characterizes all Third World Christians who come to the United States to study as conniving and dishonest. His condescending paternalism is offensive and is of the kind which is causing some nationals to call for a moratorium on foreign missionaries.

MacDonald's assertion that young people from Third World countries are eager to leave their countries and to settle in "the land flowing with milk and honey" is too broad to make without qualifications. Anyone familiar with the fierce nationalism raging among the young of the Third World knows that they are not about to immigrate to the United States en masse despite some of the real problems they are facing.

In the United States many young people have a deep desire to visit Africa for various reasons. A few are even thinking of working and settling there. Yet it would hardly be fair or valid, therefore, for one to publish that most are dissatisfied with life in America and are ready to come to Africa to stay because they are fed up with the bankrupt values of their materialistic society and its moral degeneration. The desire to travel, see the world and make one's fortune is to be found among all peoples of the world.

Instead of sneering at Third World young people who desire to improve themselves educationally overseas, MacDonald and others who think like him, should be lauding them for their desire and thirst for education and self-improvement.

The Facts and the Attitudes

As a national Christian sponsored by a mission to study in the United States, I felt constrained to examine the subject as objectively as possible. I therefore designed a questionnaire which I sent to twenty-six major mission organizations and also interviewed both American and national church leaders as well as international students studying in the United States. In the study I tried to find out actual facts and figures regarding Christian nationals studying overseas, noting both casualties and successes. I also looked at existing attitudes regarding nationals studying in Western countries.

The study showed that there are three views regarding overseas training for nationals. The first view is held mostly by missionaries. They say that nationals should not be encouraged to or be sponsored to study overseas. The reasons they give are similar to those advanced by MacDonald: (1) Many will not want to return to their own countries after finishing their education; (2) they will lose their culture and fail to relate to their own people if they do return; (3) they will not be on the same economic level with their people; and (4) they will become materialistic and lose their spirituality during their stay overseas.

The second view is held mostly by Third World leaders of the younger generation and by students studying overseas. They point out that there is a great need for trained nationals who will take over responsibilities from missionaries and for others who will take leadership in developing the young nations. All means possible must be used to get them overseas where the training is available.

In between these two groups are nationals, missionaries and American church leaders who believe that overseas study for nationals should be utilized as a last resort if the training needed is not available in their own country or a neighboring country where the culture is not too different.

Dr. Bong Rin Ro, a native of Korea and executive secretary

of the Asia Theological Association holds this view. He feels that Asians must be discouraged from coming to study in the United States. In an interview with me he said, "We have a terrible brain drain in Asia. Many Asians who come to the United States do not want to go back. Because they remain in the States, foreign missionaries have to teach in our theological schools."

In reference to Africa, Ro said, "Of course, what I say pertains to Asia where we have degree granting theological schools. In Africa your people need to go overseas. However, instead of going to America some Africans need to consider studying in Asia. There is need for Third World countries to help each other in theological education!"

Because of the divergence in thinking on this subject, different missions and churches have different policies. Some have vigorous scholarship programs and are sponsoring several nationals for study overseas while others are opposed to the idea and have no scholarship programs at all. Out of the twenty-one mission organizations which responded to my questionnaire, nine said they had scholarship programs for bringing overseas nationals to study in the United States. Twelve said they did not have scholarship programs.

The range of success of those who have scholarship programs varies from one mission which sponsored thirty nationals who, after attaining their degrees overseas, all went back to their respective countries where they are giving dynamic leadership, to another which sponsored fourteen and had only two successes. The rest became casualties. In between are missions which have had about fifty per cent success with their programs.

The attitudes expressed by the missions were directly connected with their level of success. The mission which had one hundred per cent success had a positive attitude toward sending nationals overseas. This mission writes, "The additional training of nationals has been a blessing to our work and gave an additional dimension." The mission which had only two successes out of fourteen discontinued the program, though they are still open to sponsoring one or two in exceptional cases.

What is rather interesting is that the more extreme negative responses came from missions which have no direct experience themselves, those with no past or present scholarship programs. One mission which used rather strong language in its description of what it considers the deceit of Christians from the Third World said, "We find that a few go back and are able to adjust again to their own countries' economy and culture. More go back seeming to feel that overseas study has made them superior to their fellow countrymen. They do not work well with others and others do not accept them."

It turns out that this mission, which works in several areas of the world, has not sponsored even one national for higher education overseas. Their conclusions are arrived at from hearsay.

The information from my study indicated that the number of those who become casualties is not as high as some would have us believe. Those organizations with scholarship programs are unanimous in saying that in situations where national leaders need training that is not available in their countries, they would not hesitate to provide the scholarships.

In discussing the problem of nationals who do not return to their own countries, I discovered a certain amount of confusion. I spoke with a Christian leader who believed as Ro did that nationals should not be sponsored for study overseas because of the tremendous brain drain from the developing countries. He then proceeded to quote the statistics of those who do not return. When I questioned him about the nature of the statistics, he admitted that they referred to secular people from the Third World who had come to the United States under their own steam to make their fortune. They were not referring to Christian nationals sponsored by missions and churches. God's money was invested in them so that they would go back to be leaders in the Lord's work. These, and these only, should be our concern.

It is true, as my survey showed, that although many are returning to their countries to minister faithfully, a few get sidetracked by various considerations. It is, however, dangerous to make a negative generalization because of these few. Even among them mitigating circumstances may be found. Instead of discouraging otherwise deserving nationals from going overseas by terminating scholarship programs, mission leaders should evaluate their programs to see where they can be improved in order to lessen or eliminate the possibility of casualties.

They should ask themselves where they may be failing instead of just blaming the nationals. Maybe they need to evaluate their methods of selecting nationals for overseas study by asking themselves a few questions. What qualities do they look for when considering nationals for study overseas? Is the selecting done by the national church, the mission or both? What are the cultural, economic, social and political problems faced by a national who has studied overseas when he returns to his home country?

Unless and until these pertinent questions are dealt with honestly, missions will continue to make simplistic generalizations which are not based on facts. This in turn will continue to alienate evangelical nationals as well as hinder their effectiveness as witnesses in their countries.

Criteria for Selecting Nationals

Let's look more closely at some existing standards and at those that should be used to gauge someone's suitability for overseas study. From personal experience I have come to the conclusion that some missionaries are most happy with those nationals who tell them what they want to hear. They are more at home with the passive national who does not criticize anything but acquiesces in everything. Missionaries often regard such a national as "spiritual" and are apt to bestow all kinds of favors on him, including overseas study.

The independent, thinking and creative national is often regarded as a troublemaker. Because of feelings of superiority, missionaries may find it hard to accept criticism from him. Yet he could be one who would come back to give dynamic leadership to the church because his faith is centered in Christ alone and not in the security of missionary approval.

One young African man was sponsored for overseas study by a certain mission. After his training he went back to Africa but took a job with a secular company. His Christian witness was zero. When I asked him how he came to be sponsored by a mission to study in the United States, he said, "American missionaries are the world's greatest egotists. I kept telling them that they were the greatest, and they liked that so much that they sent me to America to study. When I came back I told them where they could go."

This is an example of what happens when missions do not use proper criteria for selecting candidates for overseas study. When their candidates get sidetracked and become casualties, they wring their hands and make preposterous statements accusing the majority of national Christians of being dishonest and deceitful.

In reply to my questionnaire, one mission indicated that it was stopping its scholarship program for national Christians because the majority of those they had sponsored did not fulfill their expectations. Some remained in America. Others went back but were useless to the church.

Where there is such a high rate of failure, one is forced to look at the sponsor to see whether or not the fault may be with him. Our Lord had twelve disciples and all but one followed him to the end. And even with the one, Jesus knew he would betray him before he chose him. He was, therefore, not surprised when Judas fell away. If they use proper criteria, there is no reason why a mission or church should not be able to sponsor nationals for higher education overseas and have them all come back to give leadership to the Lord's work.

What should the criteria be? I discussed the subject with Siman Ibrahim, a Wheaton College graduate and General Secretary of the Evangelical Churches of West Africa. Ibrahim said,

> The problem is that missionaries often draw up scholarship programs and select the candidates. This is wrong. The national church knows the need and the kind of people who will be able to fill that need. Often missionaries are more impressed by the rhetoric of those who look smart and intelligent. They are easily taken in by pretence of spirituality. The national church is never deceived because it knows its own people.

Ibrahim's words are echoed by Dennis Clark, who also discusses national leadership in *Third World and Mission*. He writes, "A very important principle at issue is the source of recognition of national leadership. Does the person hold his position of eminence because of the respect of his national colleagues or because a Western Christian group selected him as a useful person?"[13]

Reginald Ebenezer is a minister of the Reformed Church of Sri Lanka. He too has some strong convictions regarding the sponsorship of Third World nationals for study overseas. In an interview with me he said,

> Sending someone to the United States to study is a great investment. We must, therefore, minimize the possibility of loss by choosing those who go very wisely and prayerfully. I would say the criteria should be that they have served in a leadership capacity in the church for at least four years. If they are going for theological education, they must have had formal Bible school training at the highest level obtainable in their own country.
>
> By sending proven leaders, you will have fewer casualties.

Their performance in school will be enhanced also because they are able to adjust their course work to what they know to be the felt needs at home.

The words of Clark, Ibrahim and Ebenezer need to be taken seriously by mission agencies with scholarship programs and by those who contemplate sending nationals overseas for study. They should rely heavily on the judgment of national church leadership. Far too many missions are casting aspersions on Third World believers when they were actually disappointed by people who never had any outstanding testimony or leadership status among their own people.

Losing a Sound Investment

Not all nationals educated overseas who fail to work within the church/mission context were selected on the basis of poor criteria. Many are godly men and women who would love to serve God but cannot do so within the church/mission context. Take this true story of one I will call Adam Mudzamiri.

Adam was sponsored by his mission, with the full backing of his church, to study theology at an evangelical seminary in America. He came with his young wife and two children. He worked hard at his studies as well as at his evening job as a janitor at the school to help pay for some of the family's expenses since the scholarship grant was not adequate. After four years he graduated with honors. His teachers spoke highly of him as well as the leaders of the local church where his family attended. They were all confident that Adam was going to be a real beacon in his church in Africa.

When he arrived home, he got together with the mission and church leaders. He could not believe it when they told him that he was going to receive the same salary as the rest of the pastors who did not have his training. He was also going to live in a three-room house without running water.

Mudzamiri protested. He pointed out that the government scale for B.A. teachers was $550 and that he would be satisfied with at least $450. One missionary in the meeting said, "It is sad that your stay in America has made you materialistic. Remember, brother, the Word says, 'Seek ye the kingdom of God and all shall be added unto you.' "

Another missionary said, "I don't see why you should not get what your fellow pastors get. After all, we missionaries get the same salaries even though some of us don't have degrees and others have several. We all receive the same stipend." Of course he did not mention that their stipend was $600 per month plus a large European style house and free transportation, not to mention a pension scheme, insurance and an allowance for each child.

Adam turned to the national church leaders, but they were not of much help. After all their salaries were paid by the mission, and they were not about to jeopardize that security.

That evening Adam and his wife spent a sleepless night as they discussed and prayed. One thing was clear, after all that studying and sweeping of floors in America, he was not about to accept $200 per month. What would his peers who were teaching for the government say? What kind of diet would he give his family who were used to a decent standard of living?

Within a week Mudzamiri found a job as a Scripture teacher at the government school at a salary of $550 per month. He was also given a European style house and a loan to buy a car.

Because of his "bad" example the mission says it is not going to sponsor any more nationals for study overseas because they will become detribalized and lose their culture. They ignore the fact that Mudzamiri gives a tenth of his salary to support the work of his church.

Some people talk about culture when they actually do not know what they are talking about. Most who disapprove of Third World nationals studying overseas on the grounds that they will become detribalized are actually not talking about culture at all. When they say "preserving one's culture," they mean that nationals educated overseas should not seek to better the quality of their lives or to enhance their social status at all. In other words they should not seek to develop as human beings but remain on the same level as their counterparts who never went to school.

One mission said that it did not sponsor Christian nationals for higher education because they would no longer be on the same level with the rest, and their fellow nationals would be jealous of them. This thinking is mistaken because people in the Third World do not all live on the same level. They are not all children who are constantly jealous of what others have. In fact, I believe Americans are more jealous of the attainments of others than Africans or Asians will ever be. "Keeping up with the Joneses" is a Western phrase which aptly describes the motivation of many Americans.

Third World nationals now know that a good standard of living is not the prerogative of the white man only. In Africa and Asia there are many who through education and hard work have attained a standard of living comparable to many overseas countries, including the United States. People would think one was crazy if after many years of study at home and abroad, he came back to live in a grass-thatched hut, herding goats and plowing a few acres by ox to stay alive. But this is exactly what some expect of Christian national leaders after their study overseas.

The educational level of Third World masses is growing at a fast rate. This rate must be equaled by the Christian community so workers will be able to minister effectively in increasingly literate societies. And if missions and churches expect to keep these educated workers, they need to provide a decent standard of living. Otherwise they will be lost to secular business which will pay at a reasonable scale. If a national has a B.A. degree, he should be paid exactly what his counterpart in government gets. In fact it would be fairer if the missionaries were also paid the government rate in the countries they work, according to their educational qualifications.

Lost for Lack of Fellowship

Some nationals come back from their study overseas discouraged because they were lonely while in America. I personally found out that American churches do not know how to
relate to the international Christian student. A church that
understands his aspirations can do much in preparing him for
future ministry. This can be done by giving him spiritual support and opportunities of service. In this way he can learn firsthand some of the methods of evangelism and Bible teaching
that he could adapt for use at home. Such experiences would
be invaluable because they cannot be obtained in a class-
room.

Discouragement can set in, and doubts about the future
can also start to enter the mind of a national while he is overseas. The close fellowship and encouragement of an understanding church body can offset these by helping him to keep
in mind his call and future role in God's work. Such fellowship
will also help in cushioning the impact of culture shock during
his first days in America. It is important that churches realize
this because the American church has often left the impression
of being unsupportive, apathetic and indifferent to the need for
fellowship and encouragement.

Lack of Education: A Spiritual Virtue?

In the early 1960s most ecumenical churches and a few of the
evangelical ones started to send key nationals for overseas
study to keep pace with rising educational standards in the
country. None of the theological institutes and Bible schools in
the country offered degrees.

When young nationals belonging to what we will call the
One Gospel Mission saw Christians from other missions going
to Europe and America to study, they started to ask their mission for scholarships so that they too could go. The leaders of
the mission met to discuss this issue.

The field chairman opened the meeting by saying, "The

ecumenicals are at it again. They are buying the allegiance of nationals by bribing them with scholarships to go overseas. Now they are turning our nationals against us by making us look bad." Another missionary said, "What do they need degrees for anyway? After all most of us don't have them and the Lord is using us, isn't he?" The meeting concluded that as a matter of policy the One Gospel Mission was not going to sponsor nationals for study overseas.

They then called in the leaders of the church, most of whom were in their forties and fifties, to explain this policy. None of the church leaders had more than five years of education. But they said the mission should give scholarships because all of them had children who had finished high school but could not get a place at the small university in the country. The field chairman strongly disagreed. He told them that overseas education would spoil their children and turn them against God. He pointed out how God was using them even though they were not educated.

He then concluded by quoting to them 1 Corinthians 1: 26-27, "For consider your call, brethren; not many of you were wise according to worldly standards, not many were powerful, not many were of noble birth; but God chose what is foolish in the world to shame the wise, God chose what is weak in the world to shame the strong."

This negative attitude seems rather unrealistic as well as unstrategic as one considers the situations the national churches are now in. The rising spirit of nationalism makes it imperative that nationals be trained to take over the work in their countries from missionaries.

In order for them to adequately take over they need training at the highest levels that the missionary was trained. To say that nationals must be trained in their own countries is also unrealistic because much of the training that is needed at degree and postgraduate levels is not available in many countries of the Third World.

To laud lack of education as a spiritual virtue is also dangerous because the Lord does not glory in lack of knowledge or wisdom. He only decries knowledge or wisdom when they leave him out of the picture. A Christ-controlled education can be greatly used by the Lord. The fact that he used Paul who was a highly educated intellectual was no accident.

The Failure to Keep Pace

When asked what he thought was the most significant thing at the International Congress on World Evangelization in Lausanne in 1974, an American churchman said, "I was really impressed with the caliber of Third World leadership. To hear those men and women from Asia, Africa and Latin America present the issues so clearly and articulately just brought tears of joy to my eyes. I said, thank you Lord for all is well with thy church around the world." In looking at the names of nationals who presented papers, led discussion groups and generally contributed to the Congress, one notices that most of them received higher education overseas.

Unfortunately these leaders are all too few. More are needed. Evangelical missions like the Christian and Missionary Alliance, Sudan Interior Mission and lately the African Inland Mission should be commended for their efforts in sponsoring national leaders for further education overseas. Sudan Interior Mission's Byang Kato, who received his doctorate from Dallas Theological Seminary in the United States, gave leadership to the Association of Evangelicals of Africa and Madagascar at a time when such high caliber leadership was desperately needed. In fact Africa urgently needs fifty Byang Katos and can use hundreds of them if missions will help by providing the scholarships needed for their training overseas.

Ecumenical churches did not rely solely on the mission sponsorship of nationals from their churches. In the 1950s when Africa was becoming independent, there were many international and United States agencies which were giving scholarships for the training of leaders of the new nations.

Mission leaders of ecumenical churches simply found out what scholarships were available for Africans from UNESCO, the Afro-American Institute, the United States government and other agencies. They then channeled this information to members of their national churches overseas who readily availed themselves of the help. Thus while ecumenical laymen came to study medicine, agriculture, engineering and other professions with secular scholarship funds, church and mission money was used to educate pastors and theologians.

The result is that ecumenical nationals now hold leadership positions in the economic, political and social life of African societies. Where issues between the church and state are discussed, evangelical nationals are conspicuous by their silence or absence. They do not have the educational sophistication to even know the issues at stake.

This was demonstrated recently in Zaire where French educated Dr. Bokaleale maneuvered all Protestant churches into the ecumenical churches of Christ in Zaire. Why were there no evangelical voices raised in protest? Sure, there was protest. It came from a group of white missionaries and mission executives meeting in Chicago. Where were the black evangelical voices? They were silent because they did not have the articulation needed to voice their feelings. Lack of education was the cause.

Six years ago, in Rhodesia, the United Bible Societies gave the responsibility for translating a new version of the Shona Bible to a team of nationals. In order to get a cross-section of opinion from different theological perspectives, the team invited leaders of national churches to send representatives to a consultation.

One evangelical national church founded by a large mission sent its best man, a Bible school teacher. When he came back he was unhappy and angry. He said to a friend, "I did not know what they were talking about. I was so embarrassed I wished I had not gone because everything they discussed was above my head."

This was true because his training consisted of primary school and three years of Bible school. He had not graduated from high school and could not have been expected to hold his own in a consultation with fellow nationals most of whom had degrees from overseas universities. Thus a real opportunity for evangelical input into the translation of the Shona Bible was lost. Unfortunately this story will be repeated over and over again because evangelical missions are slow to see the value in sponsoring nationals for higher education at home or overseas.

Risky Business

Because of the weakness of the flesh, sponsoring nationals for overseas study is risky business. Even if all the problems discussed are eliminated, there will still be some casualties. However, the task ahead is so important that a few backsliders should not deter us from doing what is right. Any mission or church still without a scholarship program for training their top national leadership is going to face serious problems soon. At the same time emphasis should also be placed on providing the same training that is available overseas right at home within the cultural context of the Third World itself.

Missionary Qualifications

8

I agree with those who reject the idea of a general moratorium on missions. At the same time, however, I also see the need to declare a moratorium on those without the highest qualifications for missionary work, especially those going to work in cross-cultural situations.

The key qualifications in missionary work are spiritual, academic and attitudinal. Prospective missionaries should undergo rigid screening to make sure that they possess these qualifications. There should be a strict moratorium on missionaries without them. In fact there are many missionaries on the field today who should be recalled home because they do not have these qualifications.

Spiritual Qualifications

Measuring a person's spirituality is an impossible task for human beings. Only God, who can see inside a man, can accurately measure his spirituality and dedication to himself. How can mission organizations decide on whether or not a prospective missionary is spiritual enough since they can only see what is on the outside?

The safe and wise thing to do is to follow biblical precedents. In Acts 13:2 the Holy Spirit spoke to the church at Antioch and said, "Set apart for me Barnabas and Paul." Thus the Spirit acted through the local church in calling out missionaries.

Unfortunately this pattern is not being followed today. Many mission organizations recruit missionary candidates from Christian colleges, Bible schools and student conventions, or through missionary periodicals and bulletins.

Here is an illustration of what I fear is becoming typical in missionary recruitment today: A young man or woman hears a mission representative speak in chapel at school. Later he goes to see a media presentation of the mission's work and its need for more missionaries. He or she takes a form and fills it, applying to be considered for missionary work overseas. Later he receives a more detailed form asking for references. If his application is successful, he is called in for an interview by the mission board. If the interview is successful, he is a missionary designate and goes on deputation. Some require that he enroll in missionary candidate school.

The church does not come into the picture at all, except perhaps for a request to the pastor for a character reference, until a source of prayer and financial support is needed. If the candidate comes from a rich family or has a rich uncle or aunt who can support him on the field, he does not even need the church.

Because of this method of recruitment, many have gone to the field who do not have the minimum spiritual qualifications. Many of those recruited from colleges don't attend church regularly and are even skeptical about the organized church. They have not learned to live under the ministry of church elders and therefore lack the discipline required on the mission field.

It is unfortunate, but true, that there are many men and women who went overseas as missionaries who at home never had the experience of leading someone to Christ, teaching Sunday school or preaching a sermon. These are the kind of missionaries whose performance on the field is causing the national leaders to say, "Maybe it would be better if missionaries stayed at home." They came as missionaries before they were spiritually mature.

Some were recruited who did not have the proper motives for going either. One young man told me that he was going to apply to a mission board because for a whole year he could not find a job or a church to pastor in the United States. He only considered the mission field as a last resort because he could not make it in the competition of American society. In talking to several young men about the possibilities of missionary service in Africa, I sometimes got the impression that some of them were more interested in adventure and in experiencing the exotic than they were in lost souls.

I also talked to several young people, however, who are indeed seeking to serve the Lord overseas in any way they can. Many of them are so well endowed with ability, talent and education that they have all chances for success in American society but feel called to the mission field. I met many such young people at Inter-Varsity's 1973 Urbana Missionary Convention.

Spiritual maturity and proper motivation can best be gauged in a local church through the Holy Spirit speaking to the church as a whole. An ideal situation would be for those who feel led to be missionaries to talk first with their pastor and church elders in their home churches.

The church leaders would then seek the Lord's face regarding the prospective missionary. As a member of their church, his own record of personal witnessing and general involvement in the church would be known. The elders would also be able to consult with other church members who know the candidate and have observed him in unguarded moments. If he is well-spoken of by the church and meets the requirements for church leadership, then the church could conclude that he is being called. I am sure the church at Antioch was not surprised when Paul and Barnabas were called because they were doing the work of missionaries and elders in their local church. A true missionary is first of all a missionary at home.

After speaking in a certain church a lady came up to me and told me that she had always wanted to go to Africa as a missionary but had not been able to go because of family responsibilities. When I asked her what she was doing in her church now, she said, "Nothing much." I hope she was only being modest. Otherwise I would thank the Lord for not opening the way for her to go to Africa because she would have done nothing much there too.

After a local church is convinced of a member's call to the foreign field, the elders can then advise him to which mission organization he should apply. In this case the prospective missionary is not acting alone but is working in concert with his church. This way the mission board only has to screen the candidates for academic and attitudinal qualifications because they know that he or she has the full trust and backing of a local church as a spiritual leader. His letter of recommendation would not come from an individual pastor but from the church saying something like this, "We the church at such and such a place, having observed and examined brother so and so, find him to have the necessary spiritual qualifications for missionary work and, therefore, recommend him to your mission with our fullest support." Such a letter would be signed by the officers of that local church.

Academic Qualifications
When I spoke at Urbana '73, I mentioned the need for missionaries to acquire higher educational levels in order to be more effective in their work. A number of people have taken me to task for some of the statements I made. Yet after seriously reconsidering what I said there, I still see no need to change my

position and, therefore, reiterate it here.

Many missionaries looked on other cultures as aberrations with theirs as the norm. The result of this ethnocentrism was that missionaries, like the Judaizers of the early church, insisted that Africans take on their cultural ways when they become Christians.

In most cases ethnocentrism is the result of a limited educational background. It is born of sheer ignorance of the nature, meaning and function of culture. After working closely with missionaries for over fifteen years, I have observed that the broader a person's educational background is, the more apt he or she is to accept and see values in other cultures. I, therefore, feel that we have reached the time when, except for special cases, a liberal arts degree and or theological training at the same level should be the minimum requirement for going overseas as a missionary.

In his book, *Frontier in Mission Strategy,* Peter Wagner differs with this kind of thinking. He feels that missionaries with educational backgrounds similar to those of the nationals they minister to, will be best able to communicate effectively. He says, "That a college degree measurably helps communicate with a semi-literate peasant is a questionable assumption."[14]

I feel Wagner needs either to clarify his statement or to rethink this subject because a good liberal arts background is a must for anybody who is seriously going into cross-cultural communications. I must insist, backed by experts on cross-cultural communications and biculturalism as well as by the overwhelming opinion of national leaders, that this assertion is inadequate. This kind of thinking has been responsible for the sense of almost pathological self-containment that is evident in missions today. It can also discourage further preparation toward good and effective Christian leadership.

Here is an example of what happens through lack of training. One day at a Sunday school rally in Rhodesia, some African women started to sing a ditty that had sprung up from among them. It had the traditional African rhythm, and as they sang they clapped their hands, swayed their bodies and yodeled, African fashion. The theme of the song was the love of God.

I watched as two well-intending missionaries came up to them. The elder shook his head, sadly tut-tutted, and said to the younger, "Do you think this is pleasing unto the Lord?"

"Definitely not," the younger said, "It is just like a beer drink." I was puzzled, for the women were just making a joyful noise unto the Lord.

An understanding of African culture and a general idea of cthnomusicology would have helped these men to see that the women's song was unique—the beginnings of a truly national hymnody which should be encouraged. Instead of continuing to sing poorly translated versions of English songs, people would then have music springing up from their inner selves as an expression of their faith.

In another incident an African church service went on and on without adherence to any set timetable. The missionary looked again and again at his watch in irritation as the service went far into the night. More people than usual wanted to stand up and testify to what God had done in their lives. When the African pastor finally started to preach, it was nearing midnight. The missionary was so irritated that he left the church and went to his house. When the service showed no signs of stopping, he switched off the main electricity supply and the church was plunged into darkness. Usually the lights at the mission station were switched off at ten, so he had given more than an hour of extra time. When the African pastor realized what had happened, he broke down and cried.

Training would have helped this missionary to understand the African's apparent lack of respect for time. He would have realized that the African has a different sense of values from his own. They do not place as much value on time as the white man does. He looks at his watch to tell the time with precision, but Africans look at the sun and tell the time by its position.

Unlike Westerners, Africans also place more emphasis on people than on programs. It is, therefore, not unusual at all for a pastor to say, "Now while we wait for everybody to come, let us sing some choruses and hear some testimonies." The service is delayed until all have come.

Today many Christian colleges have become sensitive to the need for cross-cultural understanding in the field of communications, social psychology, anthropology of religions and many others. Many Christian scholars are also engaged in research in these areas.

People with a grasp of the behavioral sciences, coupled with deep compassion, are the kind of missionaries needed in the Third World today. Mission organizations should require these vital subjects as prerequisites for all missionary candidates. Missionaries home on furlough should also be encouraged to take these courses before returning to their foreign fields. I highly recommend organizations like the Committee to Assist Missionary Education Overseas, which is a joint committee of the Evangelical Foreign Missions Association and the International Foreign Missions Association, for their sponsorship of missionary higher education in institutes and seminars where courses in these areas are taught.

Missionaries thus trained are able to witness more effectively to people of other cultures. They are also better able to assist them in thinking out their faith in reference to their cultural environments thus formulating theologies which are expressed in indigenous thought forms and familiar terminology.

This background will also better equip the missionary to cope with the complex task of ministering to a Third World which is highly nationalistic, jealously proud of its cultural heritage and very suspicious of the white foreigner, sometimes regarding missions as colonial. At the same time they will be better prepared to plunge into the vortex of social change and the often unpredictable political situations that often exist.

It is a fact that the new generation in the Third World is very degree conscious. Much attention is paid to the words of one with a few letters after his name, and his leadership is respected often without regard to his race. A college degree will, therefore, be an invaluable asset to the missionary's ministry. The years of discipline and preparation behind those few letters may also make the difference between communication that gets across and communication that is badly blocked despite good intentions.

In the Third World life is fast changing from traditional rural patterns to highly complex urban and industrial ones. Many governments, therefore, view the Western missionary in terms of his potential contribution to the development of the country. Credentials are strictly scrutinized and those without the qualifications to make them assets to the young nations are often refused visas. Those who can offer services which enhance the material and physical well-being of the people often find open doors.

Here I would like to mention the need to funnel forms of missionary activity other than through conventional mission organizations. Many countries will welcome Christian teachers, doctors, engineers, scientists and technological experts of all kinds without restricting them from sharing their faith as individuals.

According to a report on the supply of teachers in English-speaking Africa, published by Michigan State University, there are over ten thousand expatriate teachers needed immediately to teach in secondary schools in Africa. This is a unique opportunity for the qualified self-supporting missionary to give real help to the young African nations in education and to present the claims of Christ to the youth of Africa who will be tomorrow's leaders.

In their book *Missions in Crisis,* Arthur Glasser and Eric Fife devote a chapter ("Rethinking the Non-professional Role") to the self-supporting missionary. In *Missionary Come Back,* Arden Almquist also has a superb chapter ("Pitch a Tent") on the same subject. These men explore the biblical basis, possibilities, advantages and disadvantages of this kind of ministry. They all agree that the expatriate Christian overseas can be an effective nonprofessional missionary.

The era of the jack-of-all-trades missionary has approached its twilight. Along with sound biblical training a missionary needs specialized qualifications. These will enable him to meet the challenge and responsibility of helping national Christians develop leadership skills with which to meet the demands of demonstrating the power and grace of Jesus Christ to their societies at this time of rapid social change.

Attitudinal Qualifications
There is one attitude on the part of missionaries which has so angered national Christians that they now say, "Missionary, go home!" This is the racial superiority complex.

It is unfortunate but true that there are many going overseas as missionaries who carry with them racial prejudice. I know of missionaries who will go several days without adequate sleep while caring for sick Africans. They will handle the most festering of sores and give all their time to the well-being of the African people. However, these same missionaries are horrified when you even suggest the idea that they could ever accept an African as a social equal.

Some teach in the mission Bible schools that Africans were downtrodden because God cursed their ancestor Ham when he looked at his father Noah's nakedness. Apart from being psychologically dangerous to young African Christians' minds, this preposterous doctrine is heretical. The fact that Noah cursed his son's children as he came out of a drunken stupor, with a kingsize hangover, does not mean that God also cursed him. Scripture does not say God agreed with Noah and was, therefore, going to see that the curse took effect. Apart from being a false assumption the theory of the African's cursedness does not hold water because there is no proof that Africans are descendants of Ham.

In today's Africa there is no room for missionaries with even the faintest vestiges of racial prejudice. Because of centuries of racism in colonial times, Africans are understandably sensitive to racism and will not tolerate it, especially from fellow Christians.

I am afraid some in the West mistake technological superiority for overall cultural superiority and have thus failed to appreciate and even benefit from other cultures. I know missionaries who, because they look down on African culture, have not bothered to understand it or to participate fully in the lives of the people they minister to. Because of this they are ignorant of the people they work among and hold false stereotypes in their minds.

While in America, I went to see a presentation by a missionary from Africa. Among the things he displayed from Africa was a musical instrument. A lady came up to him and asked what African music was like. The missionary said, "African music is just a lot of noise. The people just shout in any way and jump about."

This both angered and amazed me because I know that African music has a very intricate structure and a unique intrinsic beauty that emanates from its steady rhythm and subtle variations. This missionary knew nothing of African music although he had been in Africa for several years. I was consoled later, however, when I discovered that he knew nothing about Western music either.

One day a missionary lady who also had spent many years in Africa came to my wife and asked her to show her how to make an African meal. A church had asked her to make an African meal for their annual missionary conference. At first we laughed at her ignorance but became sad when we realized the significance of the whole thing. After only one year in America my village-raised wife, Winnie, was able to make the most delicious apple pie and several other popular Western dishes including mulligan stew, Chicken Kiev and Beef Wellington. The missionary lady had been in our country for over ten years but had not bothered to learn how to cook even one African dish.

The missionary's superiority complex also shows itself inadvertently in his self-sufficiency. Maybe pioneer missionaries were more easily accepted because they depended on nationals for all their needs. It is possible that today's affluent missionary is facing rejection because he is so self-sufficient that he does not need the national at all.

Whereas the pioneer missionary depended on the national for food and shelter, today's missionary comes to the village with his trailer-home complete with electrical lighting, refrigerated food, cooking facilities and ice-cold Pepsi. When the people invite him for a meal, they all know that he only eats so as not to offend them for he carries his own food. Because he does not need the nationals, they too find it difficult to identify with him. This in turn hinders communication of the gospel.

In my language we have a saying: *Kandiro kanoenda kunobva kamwe.* This means, "A man asks for help from those who ask for help from him." Real relationships are reciprocal.

In conclusion I would like to point out a number of attitudes I have personally found to be very offensive: (1) A paternalistic attitude that views mature nationals as being children who need to be constantly supervised; (2) a lack of faith in the ability of nationals to take responsibility, especially where money is involved; and (3) looking on national leaders as assisting missionaries and not as serving God in their own right.

I believe that the attitudinal qualifications of today's missionary must be summed up in the word *servant*. They must take the principles of mission from the Great Missionary himself. He was a humble and lowly servant who took time to listen, to share and even to receive from those he came to minister to. He helped people without demeaning them, but preserved their dignity and human pride.

Unless present-day Western missionaries are willing to examine their attitude toward other races and cultures and be willing to humble themselves enough to listen, the future of the missionary in the Third World may be questionable.

The Divisions in Missions

9

A reason given by some for proclaiming a moratorium is that foreign missions are perpetuating divisions among African Christians. With missionaries out of the way it is felt that national churches will seek unity and thus be a more effective witness.

The idea of unity is central to the life of the church. When the hour was drawing close for our Lord to be crucified, he offered a prayer for the infant church he was leaving behind. It was not to exist for itself but to continue his ministry of seeking and saving the lost. In John 17:21 we read that prayer: "That they may all be one; even as thou, Father, art in me, and I in thee, that they also may be in us, so that the world may believe that thou hast sent me."

If, therefore, we are serious about serving Christ, we must hold the concept of unity as vital to our witness. As unbelievers observe our unity and love for one another, they will be drawn to our Lord. It is imperative that the churches of Africa and of the whole Third World consider what it means to be one in Christ and then practice that unity.

Denominational Empire Building

The first division we encounter in Africa is denominational-ism. Instead of preaching the gospel only and allowing the Afri-cans to organize their own African churches, most missions founded churches which became extensions of their own home denominations.

These denominational divisions are manmade divisions which have nothing to do with Scripture. The fact that they were imported from overseas makes them that much more irri-tating to nationals. How wonderful it could have been if in each country the churches were not named after foreign denomina-tions but after their geographical localities as we see in the New Testament. Instead of the Methodist Church, the Presby-terian Church, the Anglican Church, the Baptist Church, the Lutheran Church and so on, we would have the Church of Mhondoro, the Church of Masasa, the Church of Mpopoma and other geographical localities.

Nondenominational faith missions have been just as guilty as the denominational missions. Even though their mission-aries came from different church backgrounds at home, they did not channel their converts into already existing evangeli-cal churches. They started new denominations which they jealously guarded from being influenced by or assimilated into the older churches.

This denominational empire building is continuing today even though political colonialism, of which it was a part, is al-most a thing of the past. It seems to me that almost every church and sect in the Western world in general, and in America in particular, wants its own brand of Christianity duplicated overseas. One gets the feeling that some are more interested in extending their denominational kingdoms than they are in building the kingdom of Christ. Because of this there is much competition in missions overseas today. Here is an example.

After our church had grown to a good size, a building was

erected in a section of town. Later on another mission came to the area and started to put up a church building a few yards from ours. Despite protestations, the mission continued to build. When the new church was finished, the new missionary and his African pastor used all kinds of methods to attract our Sunday school pupils until they started to go to the new church. When we asked the pupils about this, they told us that at the new church they were given lots of candy after the service!

Competition has brought about denominational and sectarian exclusiveness which has made it almost impossible for national Christians to realize that they are members of one body with the believers in the other denominations and churches. The theology of the unity of the body of Christ and the corporate nature of the church is almost totally ignored while denominational history is expounded and glorified at great lengths.

The result is that the unity and cooperation that is so needed in Africa today is nonexistent. Each mission jealously protects its adherents from contamination with so-called false doctrines from other churches. Instead of the unity described in the Scriptures, exclusivism and polarization exist among African believers.

My own upbringing taught me to suspect other Christian groups of holding false doctrines—especially Episcopalians, Lutherans, Anglicans and Methodists! Before I could accept anybody from these "nonevangelical" denominations as a brother, I had to quiz them to make sure not only that they were genuinely born again but also to make sure that they believed exactly the way I did, even in those points of doctrine about which there is lack of unanimity among evangelicals. Some pastors of churches established by missions are even today forbidden to join national ministers' organizations and other fellowships because some of the members are known to be affiliated with groups whose background could be classed as liberal.

Solution: Not a Super-Church

Some within the ecumenical movements see the answer to these divisions as organizational unity. Interpreting Christ's prayer to mean that there should be one church organization, they believe that all Christians should be organized into one, visible, organic body. They therefore advocate establishing one Super-Church by merging all denominations.

This position, I feel, is erroneous because Christian oneness cannot be organized. The spiritual church, the *ecclesia*, is already one. In 1 Corinthians 12:12-13 we read, "For just as the body is one and has many members, and all the members of the body, though many, are one body, so it is with Christ. For by one Spirit we were all baptized into one body—Jews or Greeks, slaves or free—and all were made to drink of one Spirit."

The body is unique in the way it is put together and the way it functions. It has diverse organs and parts which work together. There is little conflict but much empathy. The essence of its unity is in its interdependence and not in uniformity. Each member is distinct but performs its task in a right and sympathetic relationship to the other members.

The churches of Africa can work together as the body of Christ without organizing themselves into one Super-Church. However, where churches seek to unite because of certain commonalities, they should be encouraged to do so.

Division over Nonissues

Much of the ecumenical theology espoused by some African Christians also does not arise from African soil. It has not come from Africans struggling with the Word of God in the context of Africa. Such theology, therefore, is inadequate in meeting the need for church unity in Africa because it is unity as defined by non-Africans.

We need an ecumenism in Africa, but it should be an ecumenism that we African Christians work out together as we seek to minister to the world in our particular situation. It must be our ecumenism derived from the Word of God to meet our own peculiar needs. By getting onto the bandwagon of Western ecumenism, Africans will only confuse themselves and their followers.

African churches within the evangelical movement strongly oppose those in the ecumenical movement and their attempts to bring about organizational unity. They espouse the position that things should be left as they are with churches and denominations maintaining their different identities.

Evangelicals are themselves badly divided by noncrucial theological positions and, therefore, are unable to form a united front in helping thousands who are in need of salvation, teaching and material help. There is so much duplication of effort where a pooling of resources could do much more in demonstrating the kingdom of God to a lost world.

A few years ago some evangelical missions and churches in a certain African country got together to discuss the establishment of a much needed theological college. It was never built because they could not agree on what eschatological position to teach even though they agreed on the fundamental doctrines of the faith. Most of those who disagreed were not Africans but amillenialist and premillenialist missionaries. I have a strong feeling that if missionaries were not there, the Africans would have agreed to have the school teach all the traditional eschatological positions and allow the students to choose the position with which they felt most comfortable. After all, whether one believes that Christ comes before or after the tribulation is not critical to one's salvation. I have read the Bible through, but I never read where it says, "Thou shalt hold the correct eschatological position and thou shalt be saved."

The present position of sectarian separatism on the part of some extreme evangelicals is, therefore, erroneous if not unscriptural. It also points out that the brand of evangelicalism that we in Africa have been espousing is not one that we ourselves have extracted from the Word of God. It is an evangelicalism which has its roots in the American Bible Belt and which may be inadequate for Africa.

The theological polarization is increasing in Africa over issues which had their origin in the West. Western liberal theologians regarded the Bible solely as a product of history and denied its divine inspiration. Jesus Christ, therefore, was to them an unusually good human being who was mythologized and nothing more.

The conservative movement was a reaction against this rationalism which denied the supernatural nature of the Scriptures and the divinity of Christ. Conservative and orthodox Protestants, therefore, separated from liberal Protestants following the injunction that believers should separate from those holding false doctrines.

I have no problem at all in understanding and accepting this divergence historically and even as it exists in the West today. Liberal Christianity which denies the authority of the Bible is dangerous because it denies the divine Messiah who died for us. Conservatives did well to separate from this rejection of the authority of the Word of God.

My problem comes when I observe African churches separated from each other not because of differences based on biblical interpretation but by issues which are in fact non-issues on the African scene. African churches are labeled "conservative" or "liberal" today not because of any theological position they hold but by virtue of the fact that they were founded by missions which came from conservative or liberal backgrounds. Western missions transferred their traditional biases and theological feuds to their spiritual offspring. The result is unnecessary division among the African churches.

Am I saying then that all African Christians and churches can work together harmoniously or that they all hold biblically sound theological positions? The answer is an emphatic No! There are very grave theological issues surfacing in Africa which probably will divide Christians there. However, these differences have nothing to do with the traditional theological issues between Brunner and Bultmann or Bonhoeffer and Tillich. I have yet to meet an African Christian who holds the rationalistic liberalism which conservatives reacted against in the West.

Africans have no problem accepting the supernatural inspiration of the Bible and the divinity of Christ because their culture is not built upon scientific rationalism. To us the world of the supernatural and the world of the natural are one world. Any missionary teacher in Africa who takes much time to prove to African students the inspiration of the Scriptures and the error in scientific rationalism may be wasting his time because African students have no problem in accepting supernatural things.

Some churches in Africa, which may have been founded by missions sympathetic to the liberal position, are themselves quite biblically oriented. In many parts of the Third World even Roman Catholics are experiencing new birth and the movement of the Holy Spirit as individuals in their churches. It is, therefore, unreasonable for missions to insist that Third World Christians maintain the traditional barriers that the Holy Spirit is breaking in their midst. Lausanne '74 offered a glimpse of this new thing the Lord is doing in the Third World when black bishops from the Anglican Church (which has a reputation for formalism and theological liberalism in the West) sang and clapped their hands together with exuberant Latin American Pentecostals as they made "joyful noise unto the Lord."

Given this situation it is foolish for African Christians to continue to be divided by issues which have nothing to do with the African scene.

Am I saying then that Western theologians have no place in Africa? No. Western theologians are needed to teach, to inspire and to stimulate indigenous theologians who need a good background in biblical exposition and the major doctrines of the faith plus historical theological issues. However, Western teachers must constantly be aware of the need to be relevant to the African situation and perspective. Thus they will teach historical Western theological issues as necessary knowledge and not as the apologetic against heresies their students are liable to encounter among fellow African theologians.

Creating an African Theology

What then are the issues which are surfacing in Africa if the traditional Western differences are not relevant? The differences arise from Africans' interaction with the Bible and with one another in their own cultural milieu. They have to do with the Africans' own interpretation of Scripture and the African theology that is being formulated.

Since African theology perceives God and his activity among men through African eyes, missionaries should leave Africans free to interact with whom they will. In this way they will be able to understand what others are saying and to react according to their own convictions. Today the few aspiring theologians we have cannot even hear each other because their Western patrons are making such a din, shouting what often is irrelevant advice from the sidelines.

African Christians need to meet together as Africans regardless of the background of the missions which founded their churches. They need to hear and understand each other and then evaluate each other's positions in the light of the Word and not in the light of foreign mission policies. If what some Africans are saying does not measure up to the standard set by the Scriptures, those who are grounded in the faith will reject it. In rejecting it they will produce an apologetic and an affirmation of what they see as truth. This will be the beginning of a much needed body of African theology.

There are only two reasons for evangelical missions being paternalistically protective of their national Christians. The first is that they have no confidence in their own teaching. If their teaching was weak, they should rightly be afraid for the churches they founded may be swayed by false doctrines. The second is that they have no faith in the Holy Spirit's power to lead the national Christians and even to teach them new things beyond that which the missions taught them.

In Africa we have three Christian organizations which seek to be umbrellas under which African churches come. The two main ones are the All Africa Conference of Churches (which is affiliated with the World Council of Churches based in Geneva, Switzerland) and the Association of Evangelicals of Africa and Madagascar (which was founded through the aegis of the National Association of Evangelicals of the United States, and is a member of the World Evangelical Fellowship). The third is Carl MacIntyre's International Council of Christian Churches which is active mostly in Kenya and is very vocal in its criticism of the other two.

At national levels we also find two organizations, the local evangelical associations or local Christian councils. For instance, in Rhodesia there is the Christian Council of Rhodesia and the Evangelical Fellowship of Rhodesia. Some individuals who are members of the Christian Council are also members of the Evangelical Fellowship and vice versa. But between the two organizations there is no cooperation or interaction whatsoever.

The same state of affairs exists in Kenya. Late in 1974 Christians in the Kenya Christian Council were at loggerheads. Those members of the Kenya Council whose churches sympathized with the ecumenical movement wanted the Council to sponsor a conference of the World Council of Churches. Others in the Kenya Council, who were sympathetic to the evangelical movement, felt that the Council should not sponsor the World Council of Churches' conferences because they were opposed to some of the World Council's aims. Christian brothers in Kenya were, therefore, thrown into disunity over an organization which is not essentially African.

Africa greatly needs an alternative to this "religious cold war" if a strong witness is to be maintained in that continent where the devil is busy at work trying to tear down the work of the Holy Spirit. I propose an African Christian Conference that will include prominent African leaders from all groups. They will be asked to articulate on paper their views on such things as revelation, the Bible, evangelism, salvation and other important theological issues facing the church in Africa. Emphasis should be placed on serious study and independence of thought. This, of course, will be difficult because many of our leaders depend on foreign-affiliated organizations for their livelihood, and they may not feel free to differ with the party lines held by those on whom they depend economically. Even though this is the case, I still feel that much can be done if such a conference would ban all participation by non-Africans.

Out of such a conference Africans will be able to recognize the true differences existing among them. Alignments will then be based on real African theological issues and not on historical paternalistic ties. The basis for cooperation will not be whether one belongs to the Christian Council or the Evangelical Fellowship but whether one has a personal knowledge of Jesus, a biblically sound theology and desire to do the Lord's will. Hopefully, such a conference would result in a new realization of the meaning of the body and could culminate in a revival which could have repercussions throughout the world.

A Problem of Organizational Structure

10

The call for a moratorium and the subsequent controversy has demonstrated that there are serious problems in missionary work which need urgent attention. For many years prophetic voices have told of the serious problems ahead, but somehow they were not heeded and business continued as usual. It was rather easy to ignore these voices and label them alarmist because most of them were Westerners.

But the problem has now reached such proportions that it is impossible to ignore because some national leaders themselves are saying missionaries should stop coming. Even though this call is loud and clear, some missions are still deluded by the assurances of national leaders who are afraid of rocking the boat.

Many more will have the rude awakening others have already experienced. They only recognize the seriousness of the problem when either the whole national church or a part of it decides to disassociate itself from the founding mission. Of course, as is customary with some, the devil is blamed for causing divisions and the national leaders who break away are labeled "unspiritual radicals," and business goes on as before.

The Key Problem: One-Sided Solutions

If a moratorium is not the answer to church/mission conflict, what is? To find a solution we need to isolate the key issue which if resolved will open the door to solving other problems. The International Foreign Missions Association and the Evangelical Foreign Missions Association correctly recognized the issue as a problem of organizational structure. They rightly concluded that structures play a key role in determining the form and quality of relationships between foreign missions and indigenous churches. So in 1971 they called the conference at Green Lake, Wisconsin, to study the problem.

This conference was very timely. The things keen missionary analysts like James A. Schurer, Arthur Glasser, Eric Fife, Bishop Dodge and others were saying were now becoming a rising crescendo with national leaders joining in.

The Green Lake conference could have had far-reaching results because of its timeliness. What most limited its effectiveness was, as I mentioned before, that it was an Americans-only conference. The few nationals attending were mostly students who happened to be in the country. They were not invited as full participants but as "resource personnel." None of them presented major papers even though many of them had strong opinions on the subject and were well qualified to speak since they were leaders in their own countries.

The structure of this conference reflected the same paternalism and short-sightedness which is making some nationals call for a moratorium. Here were four hundred American missionaries and mission executives discussing such a key issue affecting their relationships with churches overseas, and yet the leadership of those churches was not included in the discussions. It was a one-sided conference.

This certainly did not demonstrate the stated seriousness of missions to resolve church/mission conflict. A more serious approach would have been to ask leaders of national churches overseas to prepare papers from their own perspective and to present them at Green Lake. They would not have left those present in any doubt as to what they perceived as the best and most practical relationship between their churches and the missions which brought them into being. A clear understanding of the views of both national churches and missions would have been the best springboard for future action in shaping healthy relationships.

What happened at Green Lake is exactly what often happens overseas. Missions decide on the organizational structures that they are most comfortable with, and the national churches are expected to fit into those structures without questions even though they do not fit the existing needs or the social temperament of the people. Often the overseas mission board determines the structure which is then imposed on all areas of the world where that mission is working regardless of the local situation. In these cases the missionaries on the scene are powerless to change the structures to fit their situation because this requires a policy change by the overseas board.

Phillip E. Armstrong gives some sound advice. He says, "The changes taking place in the church today mean that every mission should take a serious look at its present structure. The struggle for the preservation of organizational identity must not be permitted to disrupt spiritual relationships whatever our rights may be."[15]

Decrease and Increase
Mission leaders and national church leaders need to come together to pray and discuss frankly the causes of conflict as equals seeking to do God's will. If this is not done, the situation will continue to deteriorate further with a moratorium becoming a more and more real alternative for national churches instead of just a theory.

The Latin America Mission faced this issue squarely and saw the need for rather radical changes in their organizational structure. The missionaries and church leaders worked out a relationship that has brought a stronger bond of brotherhood and trust between missionaries and nationals. Other missions need to follow their example.

Wade T. Coggins gives other options for missions when their work has been successful and a national church has been born. He says,

a. The mission may move out lock, stock and barrel and assume its work has been finished in that country.

b. It can pull out all its people and continue to send funds under some agreed-upon arrangement.

c. It can continue to operate alongside that church and find proper relationships and patterns of structure.[16]

Another alternative Coggins mentions is that the mission can be absorbed by the church. Missionaries become part and parcel of the national church, and they work under its direction.

Usually the structure of the relationship as such between the church and the mission does not determine the success or failure of the relationship. Failure comes when three key principles are ignored. The first principle I have alluded to already: The form of structure must be worked out by both the national church and the mission.

The second principle is that whatever relationship is worked out must be geared to the eventual autonomy of all the work under national leadership. The mission must not dominate the church, but rather it must decrease in its influence while the church increases.

One mission says it works in partnership with the national church. This is what they mean by partnership: The national leaders do not attend the annual missionary conference while missionaries attend and participate in the annual national church conference. The national leaders are not members of the mission's field council. Thus missionaries directly influence all national church deliberations while the national church has no influence in the mission at all except as some of them are invited to advise the field council now and then. Such "equality" soon leads to serious problems. Nationals have no voice whatsoever in running ministries like radio, literature, clinics or schools. They also have no voice at all in placing missionaries or hiring national personnel for the ministries.

The third principle is that the mission must see itself as a temporary scaffolding which will one day have to be taken down. This must not remain at a theoretical level but must actually be seen in the actions of the mission. Too many missionaries say it is their intention to "work themselves out of a job" while at the same time doing all they can to protect those jobs from being taken over by nationals.

Selective Moratorium

Along with restructuring there is also a need for missions to consider a voluntary selective moratorium. I see four possible forms for this, all of which should be put into effect. The first is that suggested by the Lausanne Covenant, in paragraph nine: "A reduction of foreign missionaries and money in an evangelized country may sometimes be necessary to facilitate the national church's growth in self-reliance and to release resources for unevangelized areas."[17]

The biblical precedent set by the first-century missionaries was to found a church, stay a while to teach, appoint leaders and then leave. Contact with new churches was by mail. Many missionaries have retarded the growth of their work by building mission stations and living alongside the church for too long.

Much of the parent/child conflict in human society is caused by parents who do not know when to let go of their offspring. They continue to treat them as children even though they have grown and are adults who should be making their own decisions. Many missions are guilty of the same thing. They continue to treat the church in a protective and paternalistic way. The best that some could probably do is to say goodby to the young church and move to unreached fields.

The second form of selective moratorium also deals with areas where churches are already established. This would require mission organizations to send missionaries only as specifically requested by the national churches. Restraint would be the guiding principle in sending more missionaries to areas where there is an active national church. Too many missionaries in one area tend to cause confusion just as too many cooks spoil the broth.

It is unfortunate that some missions measure their success by the number of missionaries they have on the field. They urge more and more young people to join their organizations and go overseas as missionaries. The result is that we have in some small countries too many missionaries who are getting in the way of national Christians who want to shoulder the responsibilities that they rightly see as theirs.

After seeing the need in the cities of the United States, I became convinced that they need more missionaries than we in southern Africa do. American Christians should also be encouraged to be missionaries among their own people of all races, instead of always being challenged to go overseas.

The test of missionary success is to be found in the results. An effective mission is one which has produced churches which are reproducing themselves. A constant call for more missionaries to a place where missionaries have been active for more than fifty years may be a sign of failure. If they could not establish reproductive churches with qualified national leadership in fifty years, they will not do it in five hundred.

The third form of selective moratorium is removing dead wood. There are far too many missionaries who have been on the field for too long without any result. There are several so-called "church planting missionaries" who have not planted a single church in the last fifteen years.

Every good business has standards of performance by which employees are evaluated. Missions should also set standards for the evaluation of the work of each missionary. Those who are not effective as missionaries should then be asked to leave and go home. If missions cannot do this, they should ask national leaders to periodically evaluate missionaries working with them.

The fourth form of selective moratorium is that of screening out missionaries who do not have the proper qualifications. In chapter eight I mentioned that because of the changing situations overseas, a missionary should have at least a liberal arts degree or theological training at the same level or both. This of course is apart from spiritual qualifications required for all in Christian service. The emphasis should be on sending missionaries with training and ability to train nationals for responsibility in specific areas.

Upon asking most missionaries going overseas today about the nature of their work, one is invariably told, "We are going to train nationals." However, upon inquiring as to the nature of their training one discovers that a good number of them need to be trained themselves because their own education was rather scanty.

In America there is a great emphasis on young people. During missionary conferences, therefore, it is the young people who are challenged to go as missionaries. The older people are let off the hook, so to speak. This is unfortunate because many times young people are the least qualified to go, especially to areas where the national church is established. The need there is usually for older men and women who have experience. They are in better positions to assist the younger churches to generate support for ministries from local resources. Older people also have much advantage over younger people in Third World countries where age is revered. Their counsel and advice is taken more seriously than that of young people.

At Lausanne '74 Ralph D. Winter made a strong case for the

need to continue cross-cultural evangelism. I am in complete agreement with his thinking.[18] Missionaries must go out to reach unbelievers in all the world until the Lord himself returns to declare the harvest finished. However, in areas where the gospel has been proclaimed and churches established, I doubt the wisdom of continuing to indiscriminately send more and more missionaries. Rather, national leaders should be given responsibility and only a select number of key missionaries should be allowed to stay in direct teaching positions.

I see the mandate and injunction for missions in evangelized areas today as being in 2 Timothy 2:2, "And what you have heard from me before many witnesses entrust to faithful men who will be able to teach others also." The need in areas where the church already exists is not for just anybody to come but for teachers at high levels.

Too large a foreign missionary force alongside national churches will retard national initiative. In highly nationalistic nations the large foreign missionary body can easily be suspected of having motives other than religious. By insisting on continuing to send more and more foreign missionaries without regard to the state of the work in a country, some missions are in fact endangering the future of those churches they so laboriously brought into being.

A Perspective for Students
11

This book goes out with the prayer that it will challenge both young and old to be concerned for missions and to be involved in them either as volunteers or informed, supporting laity. Informed churchmen should not only be discerning about which missions and missionaries to support, but they should also be in a position to influence mission policy for the better where it may no longer be in keeping with the changing world situation or where it may be using unsound methodology.

The Romantic Image
Upon reading this manuscript, however, one reader wondered whether it would not turn students off from missions. He said, "If they read it discerningly and carefully, it could say a positive word to them. A superficial or undiscerning reading could have a student feeling, well, that the weight of evidence seems to be against what missions have done and are doing and that he really doesn't want to get involved in this kind of thing."

From my knowledge of American students derived from my involvement with them at Urbana '73 and on the campus of the University of Iowa and Wheaton College, I am constrained to say this reader's fears are unfounded. Christian young people today are vitally interested in missions as evidenced by the large turnouts at Urbana conventions. So any serious book on missions is not going to be read superficially but seriously and prayerfully. If after reading this book students come to the conclusion that the evidence is against what missions have done and are doing, I doubt that the reaction would be to turn away from missions. I feel the opposite will be true. They will want to be involved in missions in order to set things right. I feel the present generation of Christian students is a crusading and activist generation which wants to get involved with the Lord's work, especially in areas where there are obvious problems to be overcome. They are looking for spiritual challenges to confront, mountains of problems to climb and oceans of difficult situations to solve for their Lord's sake.

At Urbana '73 I observed that students were fed up with the romantic and sentimental image of missions. Their questions indicated that they wanted to know the bare facts about missions, both the successes and the failures, so they could best prepare themselves to be better missionaries and well-informed, mission-conscious churchmen and churchwomen. What will turn off young people from missions today is not the honest and frank discussion of both the positive and negative aspects, but the sentimental "success story" type of presentation of missionary work which in the final analysis borders on half-truth.

If this book turns off any young man or woman from being actively involved in missions, then it has failed in its purpose. My main purpose is to encourage others to follow on and do better. The challenge and the call for new missionaries is still there. There will be no moratorium on missions until Jesus Christ returns.

This does not mean anybody can go anywhere. Only missionaries who are prepared and qualified in every way should go.
Because the church is established in most parts of the Third
World, the place where one goes has to be studied. One should
not do pioneering work where a church already exists and thus
conflict with local leaders. Where there are churches, missionary teachers should go to work with and under the direction of
local leaders in teaching the believers and doing other follow-
up and support work.

Lausanne '74 showed clearly that even though much has
been accomplished, more remains to be done. Leading missiolo-
gists tell us that 2.7 billion people have not been reached by the
gospel. Of these only 13 per cent can be reached by their near
neighbors who are Christian. The other 87 per cent will have to
be reached by people coming from different geographical and
cultural areas.

Before You Go
The challenge to go on, however, is not only directed at
Western Christians. The call to reach those still in darkness is
addressed to the body of Christ in America, Europe, Africa,
Asia and all the world. This decade and the next should be
characterized by the multi-racial and multi-ethnic church of
Jesus Christ going out as one army to meet the challenge of
world evangelization. The student seeking to do God's will is
asking him or herself, Where will I fit in and how can I best
prepare myself for the task of being involved in reaching the
unreached multitudes of the world? Here are a number of ways
to prepare:

1. Read all the missionary literature you can lay your hands
on. Bulletins from mission agencies will familiarize you with
areas of special need and also give you an idea of the daily work
and problems of a missionary. Literature on missions of a critical and evaluative nature will help you look at missions with
an open mind.

Many go to the mission field with an idyllic or exotic view of missionary task. When they arrive on the field, they can be so shattered by the real problems, failures and dreary, day-to-day routine that they immediately give up. A student needs good critical books which will remove some of the romanticism. By doing this a student who decides to become a missionary will start his task knowing full well that he is stepping into a life of hardship and conflict. He will work to be better prepared.

Biographies of great missionaries of the past also need to be read for inspiration and instruction in missionary principles and methodology. Many a missionary on the field today is there because his resolve was strengthened by reading the biography of some saint who surrendered all to win some in a foreign land.

2. Associate with missions-minded student organizations like Inter-Varsity Christian Fellowship. Many missionaries have told me that they received their call to the mission field while attending an Inter-Varsity Missionary Convention at Urbana, Illinois. In this way you can gain information or receive personal counseling and support if you are exploring going overseas.

3. Get to know Christian international students studying in your country and learn from them the needs and problems of their particular countries. Associations like International Students, Incorporated may also give you opportunities to minister to these Christian brothers and sisters from other lands. My own life was enriched both spiritually and materially by American students who befriended me during my college days in the United States. I thank God for each one of them.

4. Take an active interest in what your church is doing in missions. Ask questions. Which missions does your church support? What is the missionary budget? What are the policies of the missions supported? Is the church doing enough for missions? Are there areas that need improvement? How can I be involved in the total missionary program of my church? Can I be involved in the annual missionary conference?

5. Get to know individual missionaries at home on furlough and continue the relationship by correspondence while they are on the field.

6. Start now to support missions with your prayers and your money. Many habits started while one is a student will remain through life. The Lord may not call you to full-time missionary work, but he is calling all believers to support his work with their gifts and prayers. In Romans 10:15 Paul says of missionaries, "And how can men preach unless they are sent?" Will you be one of the senders?

7. Try to spend a summer or a year as a short-term missionary either at home or in some foreign country. I know more than one missionary who gave his life to a country after spending a summer there as a student volunteer. Wade T. Coggins says,

> Sketchy reports indicate that short-term service is a good recruiting tool. A substantial percentage of those who do volunteer work on a field during their college years end up in some type of missionary work after graduation. In addition to recruitment, short-term work usually results in greater missionary interest in the school or church where the young person is involved.[19]

I see one shortcoming in most student missionary volunteer programs. It is that students go to help missionaries in their work and not national Christians. The result is that many students who go overseas never get to know the nationals firsthand. Even though I appreciate the missionaries' need for typists and maintenance workers of various kinds around the mission stations, I feel that those coming for short terms need to be given work that puts them directly in contact with the local people.

Another point that needs to be made is that a student volunteer must never take work away from a national Christian. This was the cause of some discouragement to a national couple.

The young African man was in Bible school with his wife and children. They were having a hard time financially since both of them were in school. The husband was doing part-time work, but this did not bring in enough for the three young children they had to support. One day one of the missionary teachers at the school asked the wife if she could do some typing for the mission. The couple took this as a real answer to their prayers since the wife would be earning some money. After a week of work the missionary said to the African lady, "Thank you very much for your work. However, we do not need your help any more because there is a student volunteer from America who is going to do the work for us." This was a real blow to the couple because they really needed that job. The money would have made their student days much easier.

If incidents like this are to be avoided, student volunteers must make sure that they are not taking much needed jobs from nationals who are qualified to do them.

8. If you are at a secular college, take a summer or a year to study missions and related subjects at some reputable Christian college.

9. Be a missionary where you are. Be actively involved in leading people to the Lord. If you are not a witness now, you will probably not be a witness when you get overseas. God will call to the foreign field only those with a real love for people and a compassion for lost souls.

Conclusion

The reasons for a moratorium are not compelling. We should not immediately call all missionaries home. Christ's teaching is clear. He did not command his disciples to go until churches became self-governing, self-supporting and self-propagating. He did command us to go, even to the close of the age.

At the same time, the call for a moratorium is a serious challenge to the worldwide body of Christ to rethink and restructure efforts to reach the world's lost. The reasons behind the call should move us to bring missionary activities more in line with Scripture and the changing world situation, and to support our brothers and sisters in all parts of the world to do the best job possible of making disciples.

Notes

[1]Rackman Holt, *Mary McLeod Bethune* (New York: Doubleday, 1964), p. 45.

[2]Robert Harrison and James Montgomery, *When God Was Black* (Grand Rapids: Zondervan, 1971), p. 65.

[3]Howard Jones, *Shall We Overcome* (Old Tappan, New Jersey: Fleming H. Revell, 1966), p. 93

[4]Robert Gordon, "Black Man's Burden," *Evangelical Missions Quarterly* (Fall 1973), p. 267.

[5]Wade T. Coggins, "What's Behind the Idea of a Moratorium?" *Christianity Today* (22 November 1974), p. 9.

[6]Herbert J. Kane, *Winds of Change in the Christian Mission* (Chicago: Moody Press, 1973), p. 17.

[7]Ibid., p. 18.

[8]Ibid.

[9]James Johnson, "The Tortoise and the Hare," *International Christian Broadcaster's Bulletin* (February 1972), p. 3.

[10]Dennis E. Clark, *The Third World and Mission* (Waco, Texas: Word Books, 1971), p. 77.

[11]John S. Mbiti, *African Religions and Philosophy* (New York: Doubleday, 1970), p. 303.

[12]Ezekiel Mphahlele, *Palaver* (an occasional publication of the African and Afro-American Research Institute, University of Texas, Austin, Texas, 1972), p. 41.

[13]Clark, op. cit., p. 90.

[14]C. Peter Wagner, *Frontier In Mission Strategy* (Chicago: Moody Press, 1971), p. 61.

[15]Phillip E. Armstrong in *Church Mission Tensions Today*, ed. C. Peter Wagner (Chicago: Moody Press, 1972), p. 114.

[16]Wade T. Coggins, *So That's What Missions Is All About* (Chicago: Moody Press, 1975), p. 67.

[17]"The Lausanne Covenant," in *Let the Earth Hear His Voice*, ed. J. D. Douglas (Minneapolis, Minnesota: World Wide Publications, 1975), p. 6.

[18]Ralph D. Winter, "The Highest Priority: Cross-Cultural Evangelism," ibid., p. 213.

[19]Coggins, op. cit., p. 116.